baby&toddler
on the go

baby&toddler
on the go

Kim Laidlaw

Photographs by
Thayer Allyson Gowdy

Illustrations by
Lorena Siminovich

weldonowen

Contents

a homemade start

Whether you are at home, at a friend's house, at the park, or on an airplane, you want to feed your baby fresh food that is both healthful and delicious. Nowadays, families are constantly on the move, and mealtime doesn't always coincide with being at home, near the refrigerator and stove, with baby in the high chair. This book is your guide to coping with on-the-go meals without sacrificing flavor, nutrition, or ease.

Many people believe that making baby food at home must be difficult and time-consuming. And although it does take some effort, the rewards of feeding your baby wholesome, homemade food far outweigh the cost in energy and time that it takes to prepare it. Yes, time is at a premium when you are caring for a baby or toddler, but think of it this way: by feeding your baby healthy, from-scratch meals, you are giving your child the gift of nourishing, vibrant ingredients that will have lasting effects. Plus, with a little planning, you can make and store batches of food so that you will always have a variety at your fingertips.

Making your own meals for your baby or toddler lets you decide exactly what goes into the tummy of your growing child. Homemade food is free from additives and preservatives and also from unnecessary sweeteners, thickeners, and sodium. It is fresher than what you find in a jar or a pouch, and it allows you to offer your child a wide variety of seasonal fruits and vegetables, grains, and protein sources. It also permits you to control the texture of your little one's meal, gradually increasing its coarseness until you introduce finger foods and then move onto big kid meals. Exposing your child to delicious homemade

food will help develop good eating habits and a well-rounded palate.

This book will take you through each stage of eating, from the introduction of a smooth puree to recipes the whole family can enjoy. But it also goes a step further: it shows you how to prepare and transport your child's meals so that a busy schedule will not sideline plans to prepare and serve from-scratch food. Nearly all of the recipes in the following pages can be stored in the freezer, and every recipe is easily transported. So, no matter where you are, you can feed your child tasty, wholesome meals and snacks that are sure to elicit a smile.

My philosophy on how to feed my little girl is simple. Just six steps, repeated often, keep me sane and my daughter happy and thriving:

plan + gather + cook + store + transport + feed

I know firsthand that traveling by car or plane, running errands, or simply meeting friends at the park can wreak havoc with a child's mealtimes. The recipes in this book are not only simple to make, store, and transport but are also easy to work into your daily schedule, no matter where you are when your baby or toddler is ready to eat.

Plan

With a little planning, you can turn out a whole array of homemade baby- or toddler-friendly foods and stock your refrigerator and freezer with things your child will love. For me, planning ahead involves two important strategies: what healthful ingredients do I want my daughter to eat, and what do I already have on hand?

Offering a variety of age-appropriate fruits, vegetables, grains, meats, poultry, and fish ensures that your child eats a well-rounded diet. See what you already have on hand in the refrigerator—frozen peas, a couple of carrots, a butternut squash—then seek out recipes that use those ingredients. Plan to set aside an hour or two on a weekend day (or an evening) to churn out two or three recipes, just to get started. You can add to your stockpile once or twice a week so that you always have a variety of purees or other foods to choose from.

Gather

One of the great advantages of making your child's food is that you have control over what goes into it. Be sure that the ingredients you use are the best that you can find. Here are some tips for selecting ingredients:

Choose seasonal Not only will seasonal fruits and vegetables be more flavorful but they will also cost less than out-of-season produce.

Choose quality Select whole foods that are free from additives, preservatives, or antibiotics. The recipes in this book make good use of fresh fruits and vegetables, whole grains, and quality meat and poultry (ideally organic or free-range), and wild or sustainably raised fresh fish.

Choose organic Make sure the vegetables, fruits, grains, meats, and poultry that you feed your child are as pure and free of toxins as possible. At a minimum, try to buy organically grown fruits and vegetables that otherwise tend to have the highest concentration of pesticide residue. These include bell peppers, celery, root vegetables such as potatoes and carrots, greens such as spinach, and fruits such as peaches, nectarines, apples, strawberries, blueberries, and cherries.

Cook

Once you have thought about what you want to cook, looked at what you have on hand, selected a recipe or two, and acquired the necessary ingredients, it's time to get to work in the kitchen. The recipes in this book don't require any fancy equipment. Indeed, you probably have everything you'll need already.

Before you begin to cook, get your kitchen ready. First, wash your hands and any work surfaces with soap and hot water. Read the recipe(s). Get out separate cutting boards for raw meat, poultry, or seafood; fruits and vegetables; and cooked foods. Pull out whatever cooking tools you will need. Next, prep your ingredients. Wash all produce thoroughly, even if it's organic or you plan to peel it. Assemble all of the ingredients for your recipe(s), then chop, mince, or cut as directed and set them aside in separate bowls. Finally, follow the recipe(s) to make the dish(es). Working in stages like this is particularly helpful if you need to tend to a child, because you can stop and start again more easily.

Store

After all of the hard work you've put into making your baby or toddler food, you want to be sure it is properly stored for maximum freshness and safety. Most foods in this book can be refrigerated for up to 3 days and frozen for up to 3 months. This makes it easy to prepare a larger batch of food, which you can just grab and go as needed. For more specifics on storing and thawing the recipes in this book, see pages 22–23, 58–59, 102–103, and 136–37. To ensure safety, make sure cooked foods are quickly and completely cooled before refrigerating.

The on-the-go toolkit

Have these items packed and ready to go and you'll always be prepared whenever you need to leave the house in an instant:

Two baby-friendly spoons, and a fork if your child is using one

Small travel pack of wet wipes or a clean cloth for spills and messy face and hands

Compact or foldable bib

Fork (for mashing) and knife (for cutting foods into smaller bites)

Bottle or sippy cup for water, cow's milk, or formula (according to your child's age). For formula, have the powdered formula packed; add the water just before you go out, and then mix as needed

Favorite toy for distraction

Transport

Properly packing up food for your child and making sure you are fully organized for any outing are critical to ensuring everything goes smoothly, and everyone stays healthy.

When you are on the go, you typically have lots to juggle, including your baby or toddler! So do your best to have everything ready so that work on the road is kept to a minimum. Put together an on-the-go toolkit (see left) that you can grab on your way out the door, and pack foods in practical, spill-proof containers.

Whenever you are traveling, but especially if you are out for more than a few hours, be sure to pack a good variety of foods so that you can feed your little one a full meal. Babies under 9–12 months who are eating solids should be fine with one or two purees, as they get most of their nutrition from breast milk or formula. Toddlers need a more well-rounded diet, however. Choose foods that provide protein, calcium, and iron, in addition to whole-grain ingredients, fruits, and vegetables. Here are some examples: Meatballs (page 82) or Curried Lentil-Rice Cakes (page 83) for protein, Cucumber-Yogurt Dip (page 146) for calcium, cooked vegetable dippers for vitamins and minerals, and Mac and Cheese Bites (page 61) for whole-grain goodness.

Following are some additional tips that will help you feed baby or toddler while on the go:

Thaw foods Thaw any frozen food overnight in the refrigerator before you take it with you. Or, if you know there is a microwave at your destination, pack the food straight from the freezer and then thaw on site in the microwave.

Pack meals with care Use small, sturdy, air-tight reusable containers. I like to keep some things separate so they stay intact. Pack purees separate from finger foods or minis, keep dips separate from dippers, and so on.

Bring more than you need You never know when your little one will be extra hungry or finicky. If you are traveling for a long time, your child's routine might be interrupted, and he might not eat like he normally does.

Think about the destination Where you are going will help to determine what you bring. If you are uncertain, pack foods that won't be harmed by temperature fluctuations.

Minimize mess If you will be eating with others and wish to minimize mess, choose foods that don't drip, such as minis.

Keep things fresh If you are planning to be out for more than an hour, or if it's a warm day, use an insulated bag with a frozen ice or gel pack to keep things fresh.

Be careful with leftovers Depending on what you bring, it may not be a good idea to bring home the leftovers. Although it may seem wasteful to throw away your homemade food, doing so is better than risking the introduction of food-borne bacteria to your child by feeding him food that has suffered from temperature fluctuations or may have been left too long without refrigeration.

Feed

When you are out and about, it can sometimes be difficult to get your baby or toddler to eat a meal. Try to make eating time as regular as possible. Your child should always see meals as a special family time, whether you are on the road or at home. Here are some tips to help things go smoothly when you are on the go:

- Pop into a café and order a coffee or tea so that you can be seated at a table, ideally with a high chair, for mealtime—a setup that closely resembles your child's home experience.

- If you don't have access to a high chair, seat your baby or toddler in his stroller or in the lap of your significant other, a grandparent, or a friend that he recognizes.

- If your child isn't used to eating food served at room temperature, try to get him accustomed to it before you take a long trip together.

- If you do need to warm food, immerse the to-go container in hot water to just below the lid. Make sure to check the temperature of the food before you feed it to your baby or toddler. It should be warm but not too hot.

BABY
4 to 12 months

Introducing solids

In the first part of her life, your baby has been living off of breast milk or iron-fortified formula, and that's all the nutrition that she has needed. But at around 4 to 6 months, she will be ready, both physically and emotionally, to start eating solid foods. Easing your little one into eating solids is a big and exciting step, and the extra nutrients will help your baby to grow and thrive.

When is baby ready?

At 4 to 6 months of age, your baby will start to give you clues that she is ready for solids (at this stage that means fruit or vegetable purees or grain cereals). Watch for the following signs:

- She shows interest in what you are eating
- She holds her head steady in an upright position and can sit upright with support
- She opens her mouth or leans forward when food is offered
- She swallows food without pushing it back out of her mouth

Even though your baby is now moving on to solids, she is still getting the majority of her calories and nutrition from breast milk or formula (or a mixture), and she is still probably nursing or getting a bottle 4 to 6 times a day.

At first, mealtimes will be slow going, so as exciting as it is for you, try to be patient. Right now it is more important that your baby learn how to eat, even if that means just a few bites at a time, rather than eat in quantity. Don't be surprised if for the first month she eats only a few teaspoons of pureed food once or possibly twice a day.

Here's a step-by-step way to start your baby eating solid foods:

- **Choose a time when your baby is well rested and not too fussy.**
- **Ideally, your baby is a little hungry but not so hungry that she cannot focus.**
- **Seat your baby straight up in a high chair or an infant seat. You may need to prop her up with a few pillows.**
- **Sit facing your baby and, using a small spoon, hold a spoonful of puree near her mouth.**
- **Watch to see if your baby opens her mouth, which may or may not happen at this point.**
- **Gently touch the spoon to your baby's lips, then, when she seems ready, spoon a little food into her mouth.**
- **If the first spoonful is eaten, offer more, a little at a time, letting your baby go as quickly or slowly as she likes.**
- **Stop feeding her when she seems full, gets fussy, or is no longer interested.**

Start simple

It was once thought that the best way to introduce a baby to solid foods was to feed her commercial iron-fortified rice cereal. Although iron-rich rice cereal—or one of the whole-grain varieties now available—is still an important staple in a baby's diet, it is no longer considered the only, or even the best, way to start a baby eating solids. Nowadays, whether your baby's first solid food is sweet fruit or mild vegetable purees or a whole-grain cereal varies with the parent and the pediatrician. Many parents and doctors describe some fruits and vegetables—butternut squash, sweet potatoes, peas, bananas, apples, or pears—as ideal choices.

Introduce foods one at a time Whatever foods you choose, it's a good idea to introduce each food one at a time, with about 3 days or so between new ones. This will help you discover if something disagrees with your child.

Consistency is key At first, you'll want to adjust smooth, single-ingredient purees with a bit of breast milk or formula to a thinner consistency that is easy for your baby to handle. Initially, it should be fairly liquidy, but it can get gradually thicker as she grows accustomed to eating solids. Using breast milk or formula will also lend a flavor to the food that your baby is already familiar with.

Mix and match Before you know it, you'll be able to start mixing and matching fruits, vegetables, and grains. This practice not only makes foods more exciting to your baby but also provides a nutritional boost to her diet.

Drinking out of a cup

Once your baby reaches 7 to 8 months of age, it is time to introduce her to a sippy cup filled with either breast milk or formula. Your baby probably won't be able to hold the cup at first, so you can help her. Encouraging your baby to use the sippy cup at mealtimes will also help with weaning down the line. This is a good time to start letting your baby try sips of water, too. Hold off on the juice, however, as it contains sugar that your baby doesn't need.

Expanding the offerings

At 7 to 9 months of age, your baby is eating solid foods, and you are both becoming more accustomed to it. Once your child masters eating simple purees, you can start to expand the types of ingredients and the amount being eaten. You'll soon start to see that your baby wants to eat more solid food and drink less breast milk or formula, and you can feed her two meals a day instead of only one.

New flavors and textures

Giving your baby new foods and different textures helps to expand her palate and increases the likelihood that she will become a good eater later in life. Here are some tips for introducing new foods and textures at this age:

- Widen the range of flavors you offer your baby, including cooked fruits and vegetables such as peaches, nectarines, blueberries, plums, asparagus, beets, and broccoli.

- After you have compiled an arsenal of ingredients that your baby has tried, start to combine purees into new and interesting combinations.

- Make purees increasingly thicker and coarser. Once your baby can handle it, start to mash ingredients into a chunky puree with a fork. This helps your baby get used to new textures and accustoms her to chewing.

- Add high-protein foods such as legumes, meats such as lamb or pork, and poultry such as chicken or turkey.

- Mix a little fat like butter and olive oil into the purees to add flavor.

- Add a pinch of spices or minced fresh herbs to your baby's purees.

Know when to back off

Don't be discouraged if one day your baby loves broccoli and the next day she refuses to eat it. There is every chance that by next week she will love it again. Babies' and toddlers' appetites change day to day and even from meal to meal, and they are good at knowing when they have had enough. Some days they might eat a lot and other days not so much, but that's usually normal. Your baby will use the following cues to "tell" you when she is finished:

- Turns her head away
- Leans backwards
- Refuses to open her mouth
- Plays with her food

New skills for baby

By 9 to 12 months of age, your baby is enjoying a range of ingredients, flavors, and textures and is now ready for new food adventures, like chunks, bold flavors, and finger foods. All of a sudden, he will want to feed himself, which is a good sign he's ready for chunkier foods. It's also a clue that he is developing skills to pick up pieces of food and put them in his mouth. He is eating more and more food, too, so you can transition into feeding him three meals a day.

Chunky foods and novel flavors

At around 9 months, your baby is likely ready for chunkier mashed foods, so you can start to move away from smooth purees and into fork-mashed foods. Begin with foods you know he enjoys. At least that way you know he likes the flavor, since the texture will be a whole new experience for him. These chunkier foods will help him transition into eating finger foods. In addition to giving your baby chunkier food, you can start to feed him egg yolks and whole-milk yogurt, ricotta, and cottage cheese. It's also a great time to start adding herbs, spices, onion, and garlic to his food. He still doesn't need salt, so hold back on adding it at this age.

Finger foods

You'll know your baby is ready for finger foods when he displays the following behaviors:

- Sits on his own
- Tries to feed himself
- Picks up small objects with his fingers
- Brings objects up to his mouth
- Can mash chunkier foods with his gums

Be patient... and ready for a mess

Once your baby seems ready, you can begin to offer him finger foods. Start with soft foods he is used to eating, like pieces of sweet potato or banana. Make sure each bite is small and soft enough for him to mash with his gums. Also, don't overwhelm him by offering too many items all at once. At mealtime, present one or two finger foods at a time along with chunky purees. See the list at right for ideas of what types of food are appropriate for your baby at this stage.

Some babies take to finger foods right away and others need some time to get used to eating bigger chunks of food. He might even decide that playing with the food is more fun than eating it. But don't worry; in time he will start eating more and throwing less on the floor.

A balanced diet

Giving your little one a diet balanced with the proper nutrients is important, so offering him a wide variety of whole foods will help ensure he grows up strong and healthy. The following important nutrients are found in varying amounts in fruits, vegetables, meats, and grains.

Iron is crucial for fueling a baby's rapid growth and cognitive development, especially after about 6 months of age.

Vitamin C helps keep a baby's immune system strong and increases the absorption of iron from plant foods.

Vitamin A is essential for healthy eyes and skin and helps fight infection.

Folate helps promote heart health, build new cells, and support a baby's growth.

Complex carbohydrates provide babies with the energy they need.

Protein builds cells, muscles, and organs during this rapid growth stage. In fact, your baby will need more protein per pound of body weight now than at any other time in her life.

Zinc supports growth and promotes a healthy immune system.

Omega-3 fatty acids such as DHA and EPA are important for a baby's brain development and visual acuity.

Calcium is critical for building strong bones and teeth, and dairy is the best calcium source for a baby or toddler.

Good & bad finger foods

When your baby shows the signs that he's ready for finger foods, you still need to be careful about what you feed him. Here are some guidelines:

DO feed baby

Small chunks of soft cooked veggies such as carrots, asparagus, or green beans or cooked fruits, such as apple or pear

Chunks of banana, melon, or ripe nectarines, or halved blueberries

Pieces of whole-grain toast

Shredded semihard cheeses like Cheddar, mozzarella, jack, or Swiss

Well-cooked ground beef, lamb, or turkey

DON'T feed baby

Raw, hard veggies or fruits like broccoli, celery, carrots, cauliflower, or apples

Raisins or dried fruits

Whole grapes or cherry tomatoes

Sausages, including hot dogs

White bread

Popcorn

Hard cheese

Keeping things safe

It's important to provide the proper nutrition for your baby, but it's also important to keep her safe. Being aware of food allergies, foods to avoid (especially during her first year), choking hazards, and methods of preventing food-borne illness will help keep her healthy.

Cleanliness is key

Keep these 5 steps in mind as you are preparing meals for your baby:

- Always wash your hands with soap and hot water before preparing your baby's food.
- Make sure to wash all produce carefully, and keep raw meat and seafood separate from produce or the work surfaces used to prep them.
- Add small amounts of food to your baby's bowl as you are feeding her. You can always add more as you need it.
- Use a clean spoon to transfer food from the large batch to your baby's feeding bowl. This prevents the introduction of bacteria from her spoon.
- When you finish, discard any food left in the bowl. Refrigerate what remains of the large batch.

Practice safe eating

Babies get so excited about eating that they sometimes stuff their little mouths too full. Here are tips to keep them from choking:

- Always sit with your baby while she is eating.
- Make sure finger foods are cut into small pieces.
- Offer only a few pieces of food at a time.
- Teach her to take small bites and to chew and swallow before taking more.
- Be aware of foods that cause choking (page 17).

Allergies

Speak to your pediatrician and know your own family history before introducing certain foods to your baby. Following the "introduce foods one at a time" rule makes it easier to know if certain foods might cause a reaction; within a couple of weeks, you'll have an array of ingredients you know your child can eat without problems. The following eight foods account for 90 percent of all allergic reactions:

- Milk
- Eggs
- Peanuts
- Tree nuts (such as walnuts, almonds)
- Fish
- Shellfish
- Soy
- Wheat

If you do suspect your baby is allergic to a certain food, stop feeding it to her right away and speak to your pediatrician. If the reaction is severe, seek help at once. Possible signs of an allergic reaction include diarrhea, gassiness, vomiting, a rash or flushed skin, hives, difficulty breathing, wheezing or coughing, or swelling of the lips, tongue, or face.

Foods to hold off on

Even though you are introducing a wide variety of new foods to baby, some foods should be avoided during her first year. These include cow's milk, honey, corn syrup, undercooked meat and eggs, salt, sugar, raw-milk cheeses, and low-fat dairy. You may also want to hold off on feeding your child foods that cause gas, as they can mask a food allergy. These include broccoli, cauliflower, onions, garlic, beans, wheat, dairy products, and fruit juice.

PUREES & CHUNKS

baby's first meals

Around 4 to 6 months of age, your baby will probably be ready to start trying solid foods. At first, her meals will be more about learning how to eat than actually eating much food. In fact, at this stage, she is still getting most of her nutrition from breast milk or formula and is nursing or getting a bottle 4 to 6 times a day. But soon she will be looking forward to the different tastes, textures, and colors of her first solid foods.

Although none of the recipes in this book is complicated, the ones you will find in this chapter are particularly easy to make. You'll also be reassured to know that they are all made with high-quality ingredients. All of this is important for busy parents! When my daughter was baby, I often made a batch of food—the same ones you'll find in this chapter—for her as I prepared (or reheated) dinner for my husband and me.

Making a large batch of a smooth or chunky puree takes little time to complete and is a great way to plan for the future. If you whip up enough puree for several meals, you can store it in baby-sized portions in the freezer for the days and weeks to come. Cooking and then freezing different purees one or two times a week helps you to stockpile a variety of dishes so that your child can enjoy the diverse diet he needs. Plus, once you have an assortment of foods ready to go in the freezer, it's easy to pop a puree or two into a tote bag and head out to the park, the day-care center, or a friend's house.

This chapter lays the groundwork for your child's diet in the years to come. By finding the time now to prepare fresh, seasonal purees for your little one a few times a week, you will find it easier to continue in the future when your baby starts eating "real" food. Plus, your baby will be more enthusiastic about eating flavorful, wholesome foods as he grows up.

Storage

Once you have prepared delicious homemade food for your little one, you'll want to make sure it is stored properly in both the refrigerator and the freezer. Freezing individual portions for your baby is not only cost-effective and a time-saver but also makes it easy to have a wide variety of homemade food on hand when you need it.

Preparing baby food

Most of the recipes in this chapter call for one of a handful of simple cooking methods. The method you are likely to use most often is steaming, which avoids the loss of nutrients that occurs with boiling or even simmering. Roasting, baking (vegetables, not pies!), and sometimes poaching are also good methods for making simple purees and finger foods.

Properly storing, thawing, and reheating your baby's food will ensure that it remains free from harmful bacteria and thus remains safe to eat. Here is how to store your baby's purees safely:

- Let the prepared puree cool to room temperature.

- Transfer the puree to the refrigerator to cool.

- Remove one or two portions for baby to eat in the next day or two, pack them in an airtight container, and return to the refrigerator.

- To freeze individual portions, spoon enough for a meal (usually about 2 tablespoons) into each individual mold of an ice-cube tray or in mounds onto a parchment paper–lined baking sheet. (Square silicone ice-cube trays make it easy to pop out cubes of frozen puree.) Wrap the ice-cube tray or baking sheet with plastic wrap and freeze until firm, at least 2 hours.

- Once frozen, pop the individual portions into a zippered plastic bag. Label the bag's contents and include the date.

- You can also use small plastic baby-food freezer containers for freezing. Never use glass, however, as it can crack.

Thawing and reheating

To avoid unwelcome bacteria or a burned mouth, keep these rules in mind when thawing and reheating your baby's food:

- Place frozen food in the refrigerator the night before you want to serve it, or thaw it in a glass container in a microwave. Do not thaw it by allowing it to sit at room temperature.

- If you thaw frozen food in the microwave, use the defrost setting and stir it often.

- To avoid hot spots, reheat purees in a small saucepan or frying pan.

- To avoid burns, always test the temperature of the puree before feeding it to your baby.

In general, the fruit, vegetable, and grain purees in this chapter will keep for about 3 days in the refrigerator and up to 3 months in the freezer. Once you have thawed frozen foods, do not refreeze them. Instead, store them in the refrigerator and use them within 2 days. For more information on keeping baby's food safe, see page 18.

Purees and chunks toolkit

You don't need any special tools or gadgets to make healthful, delicious purees and finger foods for your baby. In fact, you probably have all that you need right now. Here's what I found helpful for preparing the rainbow of foods I fed my daughter:

Heavy, medium-sized saucepan

Steamer insert or basket

Baking dish

Heavy rimmed baking sheet

Immersion blender (my favorite) or a food processor or stand blender

Sturdy fork (for mashing soft foods into chunky purees)

cooked fruit purees

Easy to prepare, purees made from cooked fruit freeze well, so that you can store baby's favorite fruit into the next season. They are also perfect for mixing into yogurt or whole-grain cereals. Because they are naturally sweet, adding them to meat or vegetable purees can help ease baby into trying new savory flavors.

Select one of the following, preferably organic:

apples

pears

peaches

nectarines

apricots

plums

pluots

If you are using apples, pears, or peaches, peel the fruit. Trim and remove the core or pit from the fruit and cut into chunks. Pour water into a saucepan to a depth of 1 inch (2.5 cm). Put the fruit chunks in a steamer basket and put the basket in the saucepan. Bring to a boil over high heat. Cover and steam until the fruit is tender when pierced with a fork, 5–15 minutes, depending on the fruit.

Remove the pan from the heat, then remove the steamer basket from the pan. Reserve the cooking liquid. Let the fruit cool. Transfer the fruit to a deep bowl and use an immersion blender to process to a smooth or chunky puree, depending on your baby's age. Alternatively, use a blender or mini food processor, or mash in a bowl with a fork. If necessary, add the cooking liquid, breast milk, or formula to thin the puree to a consistency your baby can handle.

NOTE By selecting organic ingredients, you ensure that baby's diet is free of synthetic hormones, pesticides, and antibiotics. Peaches, nectarines, and apples are commonly among the fruits with the highest amounts of chemical residue, so always reach for their organic kin.

STORE IT Refrigerate in an airtight container for up to 3 days, or spoon individual portions into ice-cube trays or other baby-food freezer containers, cover, and freeze for up to 3 months. (Some discoloration may occur during storage.)

PACK IT Place an individual portion of puree in a small airtight container. If frozen, thaw it overnight in the refrigerator. If you will be on the go for more than 1 hour, place in a small bag with a travel ice pack.

raw fruit purees

When baby is a little older, raw fruit purees are about as simple as it gets and are perfect for food "emergencies" on the go. I always make sure to have a banana on hand that I can mash with a to-go fork. I've even done it on an overseas flight. Be sure to select ripe, seasonal fruit so that it will mash or puree easily without being cooked.

Select one of the following, preferably organic:

bananas

mangoes

peaches

nectarines

raspberries

If you are using a banana, mango, peach, or nectarine, peel the fruit. Remove the pit from the peach or nectarine. Slice the flesh away from the mango pit. Cut the fruit into chunks. Transfer the fruit to a deep bowl and use an immersion blender to process to a smooth or chunky puree, depending on your baby's age. Alternatively, use a blender or mini food processor, or mash in a bowl with a fork. If necessary, add breast milk, formula, or water to thin the puree to a consistency your baby can handle.

STORE IT Refrigerate in an airtight container for 1 day, or spoon individual portions into ice-cube trays or other baby-food freezer containers, cover, and freeze for up to 3 months. (Some discoloration may occur during storage.)

PACK IT Place an individual portion of puree in a small airtight container. If frozen, thaw it overnight in the refrigerator. If you will be on the go for more than 1 hour, place in a small bag with a travel ice pack.

roasted root vegetables

Root vegetables always win smiles from my little one—she loves their sweet flavor, which intensifies when you roast them. Choose two or three of these nutritious vegetables, mixing and matching them as you like, to create a customized puree that your baby will look forward to at mealtime. You can also roast extra vegetables to feed the rest of the family.

Select any combination of
the following:

carrots

parsnips

sweet potatoes

turnips

olive oil for drizzling

Preheat the oven to 375°F (190°C). Peel the vegetables and cut them into bite-sized chunks. Spread the chunks on a rimmed baking sheet. Drizzle with a little oil and toss to coat. Roast, stirring occasionally, until tender when pierced with a fork, 30–40 minutes.

Transfer the vegetables to a deep bowl and use an immersion blender to process to a smooth or chunky puree, depending on your baby's age. Alternatively, use a blender or mini food processor, or mash in a bowl with a fork. If necessary, add breast milk, formula, or water to thin the puree to a consistency your baby can handle.

STORE IT Refrigerate in an airtight container for up to 3 days, or spoon individual portions into ice-cube trays or other baby-food freezer containers, cover, and freeze for up to 3 months.

PACK IT Place an individual portion of puree in a small airtight container. If frozen, thaw it overnight in the refrigerator. If you will be on the go for more than 1 hour, place in a small bag with a travel ice pack.

steamed veggies

From asparagus to zucchini, steamed vegetables are the heart of baby food purees. Once you have mastered the method, it will become second nature to cook up whatever fresh vegetables you have on hand. Choosing seasonal produce ensures the best flavor and texture and is also more economical than buying them out of their peak season.

Select one of the following, preferably organic:

asparagus spears

fresh or frozen shelled peas

green beans

peeled carrots

sugar snap peas

yellow squashes

zucchini

Trim the vegetables as needed and cut larger ones into pieces. Pour water to a depth of about 1 inch (2.5 cm) into a saucepan. Put the vegetables in a steamer basket and put the basket in the saucepan. Bring to a boil over high heat. Cover and steam until the vegetables are tender enough to mash easily with a fork, 5–10 minutes. Softer vegetables such as peas, zucchini, and squashes will cook in about 5 minutes; green beans, sugar snaps, and asparagus in about 7 minutes; and carrots in about 10 minutes.

Remove the pan from the heat, then remove the steamer basket from the saucepan. Reserve the cooking liquid. Rinse the vegetables under running cold water to stop the cooking. Transfer the vegetables to a deep bowl and use an immersion blender to process to a smooth or chunky puree, depending on your baby's age. Alternatively, use a blender or mini food processor, or mash in a bowl with a fork. If necessary, add the cooking water, breast milk, or formula to thin the puree to a consistency your baby can handle.

STORE IT Refrigerate in an airtight container for up to 3 days, or spoon individual portions into ice-cube trays or other baby-food freezer containers, cover, and freeze for up to 3 months. (Some discoloration may occur during storage.)

PACK IT Place an individual portion of puree in a small airtight container. If frozen, thaw it overnight in the refrigerator. If you will be on the go for more than 1 hour, place in a small bag with a travel ice pack.

baked sweet potatoes or golden beets

MAKES ABOUT 1 CUP (8 OZ/250 G)

Select one of the following, preferably organic:

1 medium sweet potato or russet potato

2 golden beets (about 10 oz/310 g), trimmed and halved lengthwise

Preheat the oven to 375°F (190°C).

To bake the sweet potato, prick it in several places with a small knife and wrap it in aluminum foil. Bake until tender when pierced with a knife, 30–45 minutes. Remove the foil and let stand until cool enough to handle. Halve the sweet potato and scoop out the flesh into a deep bowl, discarding the skin.

To bake the golden beets, place them, cut side down, in a baking dish just large enough to hold them in a single layer. Add ¼ cup (2 fl oz/ 60 ml) water. Cover the baking dish with foil. Bake until tender when pierced with a knife, 50–60 minutes. Remove the foil and let stand until cool enough to handle. Slip off and discard the skins of the beets and cut into chunks.

Place the sweet potato flesh or beet chunks in a deep bowl. Use an immersion blender to process to a smooth or chunky puree, depending on your baby's age. Alternatively, use a blender or mini food processor, or mash in a bowl with a fork. If necessary, add breast milk, formula, or water to thin the puree to a consistency your baby can handle.

STORE IT Refrigerate sweet potato or beet puree in an airtight container for up to 3 days, or spoon individual portions into baby-food freezer containers, cover, and freeze for up to 3 months. (Some discoloration may occur during storage.)

PACK IT Place an individual portion of puree in a small airtight container. If frozen, thaw it overnight in the refrigerator. If you will be on the go for more than 1 hour, place in a small bag with a travel ice pack.

sautéed greens

Leafy greens are chock-full of vitamins and bountiful in folate and antioxidants, making them dietary powerhouses for anyone older than about seven months (the presence of nitrates can make them slightly riskier for younger babies). If your baby does not like the deep flavor of greens, mix this sauté with a different puree to accustom your baby to the flavor.

Select 1 small bunch of the following, preferably organic:

spinach

Swiss chard

kale

collard greens

1 teaspoon olive oil

Trim the greens of any fibrous stalks. Rinse the greens well, then roughly chop. In a frying pan over medium-low heat, add the greens and sauté, stirring often, until they release their liquid and become tender, about 3 minutes for spinach, 5 minutes for chard, and 10 minutes for kale or collard greens. If the greens start to look dry during cooking, add a few teaspoons of water.

Drain the greens, reserving any cooking liquid. Finely chop the greens, or put them in a deep bowl and use an immersion blender to process to a smooth puree. Alternatively, use a blender or mini food processor. If necessary, add cooking liquid, breast milk, or formula to thin the puree to a consistency your baby can handle.

STORE IT Refrigerate in an airtight container for up to 3 days, or spoon individual portions into ice-cube trays or other baby-food freezer containers, cover, and freeze for up to 3 months.

PACK IT Place an individual portion of puree in a small airtight container. If frozen, thaw it overnight in the refrigerator. If you will be on the go for more than 1 hour, place in a small bag with a travel ice pack.

roasted winter squash

When winter squashes and pumpkins are plentiful in autumn, make this versatile puree and store it for the coming months. This was one of my daughter's first foods, and even when she's being extra picky, I can usually get her to eat this wholesome vegetable packed with antioxidants, vitamins A and C, and fiber.

MAKES ABOUT 2 CUPS (1 LB/500 G)

1 small butternut or acorn squash, Sugar Pie pumpkin, or other winter squash, about 1 lb (500 g)

Preheat the oven to 375°F (190°C). Using a heavy, sharp knife, cut the squash in half lengthwise. Using a large metal spoon, scrape out the seeds and fibrous strings from the cavities and discard.

Put the squash halves, cut side down, in a shallow baking pan or dish. Pour water into the pan to come ¼ inch (6 mm) up the sides of the squash. Roast the squash until very tender, 45–60 minutes. Remove from the oven and let cool.

Using the spoon, scoop out the flesh of the squash into a deep bowl, discarding the skin. Use an immersion blender to process to a smooth or chunky puree, depending on your baby's age. Alternatively, use a blender or mini food processor, or mash in a bowl with a fork. If necessary, add breast milk, formula, or water to thin the puree to a consistency your baby can handle.

STORE IT Refrigerate in an airtight container for up to 3 days, or spoon individual portions into ice-cube trays or other baby-food freezer containers, cover, and freeze for up to 3 months.

PACK IT Place an individual portion of puree in a small airtight container. If frozen, thaw it overnight in the refrigerator. If you will be on the go for more than 1 hour, place in a small bag with a travel ice pack.

fruit & veggie combos

Adding fruit to a vegetable puree, especially one that isn't naturally sweet, can make a variety of vegetables more palatable to babies. Apples and pears are the most common choices for mixing with vegetables, but experiment with different fruit and vegetable flavor combinations to see what your baby likes.

banana + avocado

apple +
butternut squash

beet + blueberry

pear + parsnip

ground poultry or meat

Meat is an excellent source of protein for baby, and red meat, such as lamb and beef, or even pork, veal, or dark-meat poultry, offers plenty of much-needed iron. Because ground meat is often bland, it is a good addition to savory vegetable purees. Or, experiment with fruit purees, such as lamb with apricot, or pork or chicken with apple.

MAKES ABOUT 1 CUP (8 FL OZ/250 ML)

Select ½ lb (250 g) of the following:

ground dark-meat chicken

ground dark-meat turkey

lean ground lamb

lean ground beef

In a nonstick frying pan over medium heat, combine the meat and ¼ cup (2 fl oz/60 ml) water. Cook, breaking up the meat and stirring constantly, until the meat is cooked through and no longer pink, about 5 minutes. Let cool, then drain and reserve the cooking juices.

Transfer the meat to a food processor and pulse to a smooth or coarse puree, depending on your baby's age and chewing ability. Add cooking juices as needed to moisten the meat.

STORE IT Refrigerate in an airtight container for 1 day, or spoon individual portions into ice-cube trays or other baby-food freezer containers, cover, and freeze for up to 3 months.

PACK IT Place an individual portion of puree in a small airtight container. If frozen, thaw it overnight in the refrigerator. If you will be on the go for more than 30 minutes, place in a small bag with a travel ice pack.

braised chicken or meat

Braising chicken, pork, and beef renders it tender and succulent, perfect for a baby who is starting to experiment with new textures. These cooked meats also provide protein, iron, and fat, all of which are important for baby's brain development. Finely mince or puree the chicken, pork, or beef for the younger ones, or shred it when baby is ready for finger foods.

MAKES ABOUT 1 CUP (8 FL OZ/250 ML)

Select ½ lb (250 g) of the following:

boneless, skinless chicken thighs

boneless pork shoulder or pork butt, cut into chunks

boneless beef stew meat, cut into chunks

2 teaspoons olive oil

½ cup (4 fl oz/125 ml) low-sodium chicken, vegetable, or beef stock or water

In a small, heavy pot or saucepan over medium-high heat, warm the oil. Add the meat to the pan. Cook, turning, until browned, about 4 minutes. Add the stock and stir to scrape up any browned bits on the bottom of the pan.

Bring the liquid almost to a boil, then reduce the heat to low, cover, and simmer, stirring every so often, until the meat is very tender. The chicken will take about 30 minutes, and the pork and beef will take about 1 hour. Let cool, then drain and reserve the cooking juices.

Depending on your baby's age and chewing ability, shred or finely chop the meat to a size your baby can handle. Or, transfer the meat to a food processor and pulse to a smooth or coarse puree, adding cooking juices as needed to moisten the meat.

STORE IT Refrigerate in an airtight container for 1 day, or spoon individual portions into ice-cube trays or other baby-food freezer containers, cover, and freeze for up to 3 months.

PACK IT Place an individual portion of puree in a small airtight container. If frozen, thaw it overnight in the refrigerator. If you will be on the go for more than 30 minutes, place in a small bag with a travel ice pack.

adding herbs & spices

To expand your baby's flavor palate, add a pinch of minced fresh herbs or spices to her fruit or vegetable puree. Start slowly to get baby used to the taste, and then experiment by adding a bit more, or by trying mixtures of herbs or spices.

ideas

peach + basil

avocado + cilantro

pea + mint

zucchini + oregano

sweet potato + rosemary

green bean + thyme

carrot + mild chili powder

butternut squash + cinnamon

cauliflower + coriander

beet + cumin

pear + ginger

banana + nutmeg

basil

cumin

thyme

coriander

oregano

ginger

cinnamon

cilantro

nutmeg

rosemary

mint

mild chili powder

brown rice

MAKES ABOUT 1½ CUPS (12 FL OZ/375 ML)

½ cup (3½ oz/105 g) small-grain brown rice

1 cup (8 fl oz/250 ml) water or low-sodium chicken or vegetable broth

In a small saucepan over medium heat, combine the rice and water. Bring to a boil, reduce the heat to low, cover, and simmer gently until the liquid is absorbed and the rice is tender, about 50 minutes. Remove from the heat and let stand, covered, for 10 minutes.

Transfer the cooked rice to a blender or food processor along with 2–4 tablespoons water and process to a smooth or coarse puree, depending on your baby's age and chewing ability. Or, you can blend it with a vegetable or fruit puree to smooth it out.

barley

MAKES ABOUT 1½ CUPS (12 FL OZ/375 ML)

½ cup (3½ oz/105 g) pearl barley

1 cup (8 fl oz/250 ml) water or low-sodium chicken or vegetable broth

In a small saucepan over medium heat, combine the barley and water. Bring to a boil, reduce the heat to low, cover, and simmer gently until the barley is tender, about 30 minutes. Remove from the heat and let stand, covered, for 10 minutes. Drain off any excess water.

Transfer the cooked barley to a blender or food processor along with 2–4 tablespoons water and process to a smooth or coarse puree, depending on your baby's age and chewing ability. Or, you can blend it with a vegetable or fruit puree to smooth it out.

STORE THEM Refrigerate cooked brown rice or barley in an airtight container for up to 2 days, or spoon individual portions into ice-cube trays or other freezer containers, cover, and freeze for up to 3 months.

PACK THEM Place an individual portion of grains in a small airtight container. If frozen, thaw it overnight in the refrigerator.

oatmeal

MAKES ABOUT ¾ CUP (6 FL OZ/180 ML)

¼ cup (¾ oz/20 g)
old-fashioned rolled oats

¾–1 cup (6–8 fl oz/
180–250 ml) water

In a small saucepan over medium heat, combine the oats and water. Bring to a boil, reduce the heat to low, and simmer gently, stirring occasionally, until the liquid is absorbed and the oats are tender, 5–10 minutes. Remove from the heat and let cool to lukewarm.

Transfer the cooked oatmeal to a blender or food processor along with a few teaspoons of water and process to a smooth or coarse puree, depending on your baby's age and chewing ability. Or, you can blend it with a fruit puree to smooth it out.

quinoa

MAKES ABOUT 1½ CUPS (12 FL OZ/375 ML)

½ cup (3 oz/90 g) quinoa

1 cup (8 fl oz/250 ml)
water or low-sodium
chicken or vegetable broth

In a small saucepan over medium heat, combine the quinoa and water. Bring to a boil, reduce the heat to low, cover, and simmer gently until the liquid is absorbed and the quinoa is tender, 15–20 minutes. Remove from the heat and let stand, covered, for 10 minutes.

Transfer the cooked quinoa to a blender or food processor along with 1–2 tablespoons of water and process to a smooth or coarse puree, depending on your baby's age and chewing ability. Or, you can blend it with a vegetable or fruit puree to smooth it out.

STORE THEM Refrigerate cooked oatmeal or quinoa in an airtight container for up to 2 days, or spoon individual portions into ice-cube trays or other freezer containers, cover, and freeze for up to 3 months.

PACK THEM Place an individual portion of grains in a small airtight container. If frozen, thaw it overnight in the refrigerator.

fun combos

Now that you have lots of recipes—for steamed, roasted, and sautéed vegetables; for fruit purees; and for proteins and grains—here are some fun ways to combine them.

southern-style pork

shredded or finely chopped braised pork,
peach puree + braised greens + cooked barley

curry chicken and veggies

shredded or finely chopped cooked chicken,
sweet potato or carrot puree + apricot puree + cooked brown rice
drizzle of coconut milk + pinch of mild curry powder

taco bowl

cooked ground turkey + mashed avocado
mild roasted-tomato salsa + pinch of ground cumin

baby's beef stew

shredded or finely chopped cooked beef + carrot puree
pea puree + pear puree + steamed quinoa

thanksgiving delight

cooked ground turkey + sweet potato puree
applesauce + pinch of minced fresh sage

homemade yogurt

Making your own yogurt might sound hard (and does require a yogurt maker), but it actually takes very little time and effort, and once you—and your baby—taste this tangy, creamy version, you will not want to go back to store-bought. Plus, making your own yogurt means you can control the fruit and sugar content, adding your own wholesome fruit purees.

MAKES ABOUT SEVEN ½-CUP (4-OZ/125-G) JARS

4 cups (32 fl oz/1 l) whole milk

¼ cup (1 oz/30 g) organic nonfat dry milk

1 packet (⅓ oz/10 g) yogurt culture

In a saucepan over medium heat, warm the whole milk to 185°F (90°C). Use an instant-read thermometer to read the temperature. Remove from the heat and set aside to cool to 115°F (46°C).

In a glass measuring pitcher, whisk together the dry milk and yogurt culture with about ¼ cup (2 fl oz/60 ml) of the cooled whole milk. The mixture will be slightly lumpy. Pour it into the saucepan with the remaining whole milk and whisk to combine. Strain the mixture into a large glass measuring pitcher or other pitcher. Fill the jars of your yogurt maker, dividing the milk mixture evenly.

Place the jars in the yogurt maker, turn it on, and let sit for at least 4 hours or up to 6 hours. The longer it sits, the thicker the yogurt will become. Screw on the lids and place in the refrigerator to cool for at least 2 hours before serving. The yogurt will keep in the refrigerator for up to 2 weeks.

NOTE All sorts of healthful ingredients can be mixed into yogurt. Try cooked or raw fruit purees or mashed or chopped fruit. Blueberries, raspberries, bananas, or peaches (or a combination) are favorites at our house. (Yogurt is also a great vehicle for prune puree when baby is constipated.) Look for yogurt culture in well-stocked supermarkets and specialty food stores.

smoothies

Instead of transporting juice, which doesn't contain the natural fiber of whole fruits, pack vitamin-rich fruit smoothies for outings. The addition of whole-milk yogurt provides extra calcium and protein. Here is an array of colorful blends that kids will find both eye-catching and yummy. Put them in screw-topped jars for easy toting.

purple

In a blender, combine ½ cup (2 oz/60 g) blueberries; 4 fresh cherries, pitted; ½ frozen banana, sliced; and ¼ cup (2 oz/60 g) plain whole-milk Greek yogurt. Cover and blend on high speed until smooth.

pink

In a blender, combine 4 stemmed strawberries, sliced; ½ frozen banana, sliced; and ¼ cup (2 oz/60 g) plain whole-milk Greek yogurt. Cover and blend on high speed until smooth.

green

In a blender, combine ½ cup
(1 oz/30 g) chopped spinach;
½ frozen banana, sliced;
2 tablespoons applesauce; and
¼ cup (2 oz/60 g) plain whole-milk
Greek yogurt. Cover and blend
on high speed until smooth.

orange

In a blender, combine ½ cup
(3 oz/90 g) peeled and
chopped peach; ½ frozen
banana, sliced; and ¼ cup
(2 oz/60 g) plain whole-milk
Greek yogurt. Cover and blend
on high speed until smooth.

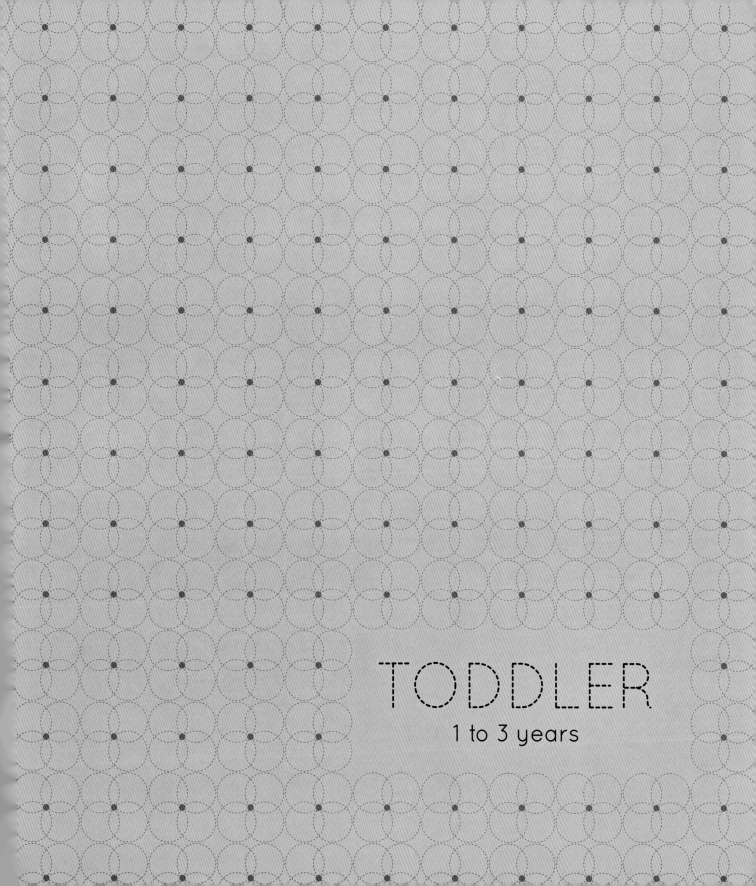

TODDLER

1 to 3 years

Fueling a growing body

It's hard to believe how quickly a year can go by. By 12 to 18 months of age, your baby has transformed into a determined little person, full of energy and personality. Quite possibly she is walking or getting ready to start walking, and her eating habits have gradually transitioned into consuming more and more finger foods and coarser-textured purees. To keep up with all that energy, offer three meals a day, plus a couple of snacks if she still seems hungry.

A changing diet

At 12 months of age, your baby has started eating more and more solid food, and breast milk or formula is no longer her main source of nutrition. She has probably grown interested in what you are eating, and you can start introducing her to all kinds of new tastes. Foods that you might not have fed her previously—whole eggs, cow's milk, fish, wheat, soy, and strawberries—are now fair game.

Breast milk is still an excellent source of nutrition at 12 months of age, but if your baby is drinking formula, it's time to transition to cow's milk (assuming your child isn't sensitive to lactose). Milk (or breast milk) is no longer her main source of nutrition and can now be considered a beverage. She now needs only about 2 cups (16 fl oz/500 ml) of milk per day. Some babies take to cow's milk without a problem, and some just don't like the taste. You can introduce cow's milk by adding a little of it to her prepared formula and then gradually increasing the amount.

In addition to providing more variety in your toddler's diet, it's important to meet her nutrition needs, so that she will continue to grow healthy and strong and maintain all that energy. Here are the nutrients that she needs:

Fat- and protein-rich foods, such as whole milk, cheese, yogurt, meat, poultry, eggs, and fish, will aid growth and brain development.

Complex carbohydrates, such as beans and whole-grain breads and pastas, will provide your little one with energy.

Iron fuels your toddler's growing body and brain, so it is important that she gets enough through meat, fish, and dark-meat poultry or iron-fortified cereals.

Say goodbye to the bottle

If you haven't done so already, now is the ideal time to transition from the much-loved bottle to a sippy cup. In general, drinking from a cup will decrease the amount of milk your toddler consumes, which means she will have more room in her tummy for nutritious food.

An independent attitude

Although your toddler needs food for energy, she might be eating more erratically at this age. This is normal. As long as you offer her a variety of healthful foods, she will probably eat what she needs over the course of a few days, rather than meal to meal. (If your child is extremely picky or losing weight, you should speak to your pediatrician.) When your toddler starts walking, you might find that she wants to walk around nibbling on her food. To prevent choking and support good table habits, encourage her to sit down when she is eating, even if you are on the go. She's also more and more interested in trying to feed herself. Help her learn to use her toddler-sized utensils by practicing with chunky foods that hold together well.

Tempting a toddler

By 18 months, your little one is well on her way to becoming a kid. There's also a good chance that she's headstrong, has a short attention span, and has become choosy about food. Even if your child ate everything when she was a baby, at the toddler stage she can be infuriatingly picky. Here are some of my favorite tips and tricks for making mealtime peaceful instead of a battleground.

Let her choose Let your little one pick what she eats from a variety of foods on her plate. Giving her a sense of choice is empowering. Also, toddlers are often interested in helping choose the raw ingredients at the market and then "participating" in preparing them.

Offer new foods Along with the foods and dishes that she is used to, try to give her something new every day to keep things interesting. Don't be dismayed if she rejects it at first. Just keep offering it every so often and chances are she'll learn to like it.

Sneak in the good stuff If your toddler refuses green vegetables (like mine sometimes does), add them to something she does like. Tucked into a quesadilla or stirred into mac and cheese, vegetables like sautéed spinach, shredded

carrots, or steamed peas will become favorites once again.

Keep up the routine Children like consistency, so it's a good idea to set times for meals and times for snacks. Even when you are on the go, stopping for snack time will help your child feel secure and keep up her energy until mealtime.

Dunk her dinner Toddlers like to dunk just about anything into a sauce, puree, or dip. Make eating into a fun game with a variety of dips and dippers (pages 138–153). Or, try Mac & Cheese Bites (page 61) dipped in marinara sauce, Roasted Root Vegetables (page 28) dipped in yogurt, or your child's favorite combinations.

Mix it up Who says you have to eat fruity oatmeal or scrambled eggs for breakfast when they are just as good for supper? And mini grilled cheese sandwiches (page 132) make an excellent start to the day.

Toddler snacks on the go

None of these simple, wholesome snacks requires a recipe; they are just easy grab-and-go ideas!

Avocados

Bananas

Baked sweet potatoes

Hard-boiled egg

Peanut butter and cracker "sandwiches"

Steamed peas

Strawberries

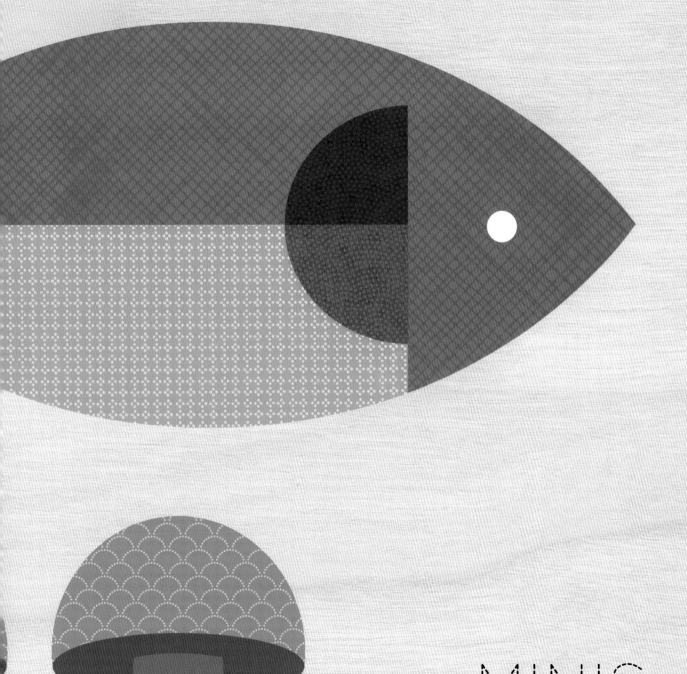

MINIS

endless variety

The recipes in this chapter are all about packing nutritious ingredients into bite-sized meals that are perfect for travel, good for your growing toddler, and fun to eat. They are also about making sure that your child is exposed to lots of variety every day. That means using all kinds of vegetables, fruits, meats, poultry, and seafood to make everything from mini frittatas, quiches, meat loaves, and pastas to muffins, biscuits, and savory cakes.

One week my daughter loves peas and the next week she won't touch them. It happens with all kinds of ingredients and dishes that I prepare. But I find that if I keep giving her variety, trying ingredients in different ways, and continue to offer her the ingredients she once loved and is currently rejecting, she often comes back to them and loves them once again.

In this chapter you'll find recipes that are not only good for increasing diversity in your child's diet but will also save you time and effort because of their great versatility. Foundation recipes like Mac & Cheese Bites (page 61), Frittata Bites (page 69), and mini quiches (page 77) can be made with just about any type of chopped vegetable, poultry, meat, or cheese that you have on hand and that you think your child might enjoy. Once you master these basic recipes, you'll be well on your way to creating nutritious meals that travel well and your toddler will like.

Seasoning Savvy

Your toddler can eat a variety of foods now, but he can still do without a lot of added salt or sugar. Instead, try adding small amounts of herbs, spices, or seasonings like garlic and mild

chiles to see if he enjoys the new flavors. Increase the quantity gradually over time so you can check for his reaction. Adding different flavors when your child is young will help broaden his palate as he grows. For more ideas on adding herbs and spices, turn to page 42.

Storing mini meals

Every recipe in this chapter can be stored in the freezer, which will make your life a lot easier

Minis toolkit

You don't need fancy equipment to make the recipes in this chapter. In fact, you probably already have any necessary cookware.

24-cup mini muffin pan

Standard 12-cup muffin pan

Rimmed baking sheet

Saucepan

Whisk and wooden spoon

Box grater-shredder

when you are trying to figure out what to pack for feeding on the road. In addition, if you prepare one or two recipes from this chapter every week, before you know it you will have a variety of protein- and vegetable-packed homemade food at your fingertips.

It's important to store, thaw, and reheat your toddler's food properly to ensure that it stays safe. The foods in this chapter will typically keep for about 3 days in the refrigerator and up to 3 months in the freezer. Do not refreeze thawed frozen foods. Instead, store them in the refrigerator and use them within 2 days.

- Once the minis are cooked, let them cool slightly in or on the pan, then remove them from the pan and let them cool to room temperature.

- Set aside one or two portions in the refrigerator for your little one to eat in the next day or two.

- Place the remaining minis on a small baking sheet, cover with plastic wrap, and freeze until firm, at least 2 hours.

- Once frozen, transfer the minis to an airtight container or zippered plastic bag, label it with the contents and the date, and return to the freezer.

- To thaw frozen food, place it in the refrigerator the night before you want to use it, or thaw it in a glass container in the microwave. Do not thaw it by allowing it to sit at room temperature.

- If you thaw the food in a microwave, be sure to use the defrost mode to avoid hot spots. If you are taking the food with you, thaw it just to room temperature, then store in an airtight container in the refrigerator until you are ready to go.

- Always test the temperature of the food before feeding it to your toddler.

Make-ahead tips

Spending a little time—even 10 minutes while baby is napping—to prepare for the coming days' meals will pay off during a busy week.

- Wash and chop vegetables and store them in small bags in the refrigerator.

- Precook pasta, then drain and cool under cold running water. Mix it with a little oil and store it in a zippered plastic bag in the refrigerator for up to 3 days.

- Shred cheese in a food processor or with a box grater-shredder and keep it in an airtight container in the refrigerator.

- After dinner, cut or shred leftover meat, poultry, or fish into small pieces and reserve in a zippered plastic bag in the refrigerator for up to 2 days.

- Wash and spin dry spinach or other greens as soon as you bring them home from the store.

- Cook a batch of brown rice, barley, or quinoa (pages 44–45), let cool to room temperature, then store in an airtight container in the refrigerator for up to 3 days.

- Make a double batch of Mini Turkey Meat Loaves (page 81) or Meatballs (page 82) and freeze the second batch to use another week.

- Prepare a batch of Master Muffin Mix (page 87) to have on hand for quick baked goods.

mac & cheese bites

This is a staple in our house, and I always make sure I have a batch stored in the freezer. These tasty bites are perfect to pop into a container and take anywhere, and they are a great size for little hands. They are also ideal vehicles for nutritious ingredients like chopped cooked chicken or vegetables. Just stir them into the mix before baking.

MAKES ABOUT 12 BITES

Olive oil cooking spray

½ cup (2 oz/60 g) whole-wheat elbow macaroni

1½ teaspoons unsalted butter

1½ teaspoons all-purpose flour

¼ cup (2 fl oz/60 ml), whole milk, warmed

½ cup (2 oz/60 g) shredded sharp white Cheddar cheese

1 tablespoon grated Parmesan cheese

1 large egg, beaten

Preheat oven to 375°F (190°C). Spray a 24-cup mini muffin pan with cooking spray.

Bring a saucepan filled with water to a boil over high heat. Add the macaroni, reduce heat to medium, and cook until al dente, about 7 minutes or according to package directions. Drain the pasta. You should have about 1 cup (4½ oz/140 g).

In the same saucepan over medium-low heat, melt the butter. Add the flour and whisk until smooth. Slowly add the milk while whisking constantly, until smooth. Continuing to whisk, slowly add the cheeses until smooth. Add the macaroni to the cheese sauce and stir to combine. Add the egg to the pasta and mix well.

Spoon the pasta mixture into about 12 of the prepared muffin cups, dividing evenly and filling the cups. Bake until crisp and browned around the edges and bubbling, about 10 minutes. Allow to cool in the pan for about 10 minutes before removing (use a small knife to help dislodge them if necessary).

STORE IT Refrigerate in an airtight container for up to 3 days, or seal in a zippered plastic bag and freeze for up to 3 months.

PACK IT Thaw 2 or 3 mac & cheese bites, if necessary, then pack in a small airtight container. If you are on the go for more than 1 hour, place in a small bag with a travel ice pack.

mac &
cheese fun

In our house, mac and cheese is just the starting point for a whole array of delicious, cheese-laden pasta dishes. Here are four of our favorites, all of them a great way to introduce new flavors in a familiar package. Feel free to put together your own combinations, drawing on what your toddler likes to eat.

meaty

Follow the recipe for Mac & Cheese Bites on page 61. Add ¼ cup (1½ oz/45 g) shredded or finely chopped cooked chicken, pork, or beef to the cheese sauce along with the cooked macaroni.

cauliflower or broccoli

Follow the recipe for Mac & Cheese Bites on page 61. Add ¼ cup (1 oz/30 g) finely chopped cooked broccoli or cauliflower (or a combination) to the cheese sauce along with the cooked macaroni.

roasted butternut squash

Follow the recipe for Mac & Cheese Bites on page 61. Add ¼ cup (2 oz/60 g) finely diced or mashed roasted butternut squash (page 36) to the cheese sauce along with the cooked macaroni.

spinach

Follow the recipe for Mac & Cheese Bites on page 61. Add ¼ cup (2 oz/60 g) chopped cooked spinach(page 35) to the cheese sauce along with thecooked macaroni.

pasta primavera bites

Packed with vegetables, these cheese-rich pasta bites are a great way to make sure your toddler, no matter how picky, eats a good amount of healthful vegetables. Because the mixture includes egg—which adds a little more protein—the bites hold together well. If you like, trade out the mozzarella for Monterey jack or Swiss.

MAKES ABOUT 16 BITES

Olive oil cooking spray

Scant 1 cup (3 oz/90 g) whole-wheat fusilli or other pasta shape

¼ cup (1 oz/30 g) finely chopped broccoli or cauliflower

3 tablespoons shredded carrot

2 tablespoons frozen petite peas

1 tablespoon unsalted butter

¼ teaspoon minced garlic (optional)

2 teaspoons all-purpose flour

⅓ cup (3 fl oz/80 ml) whole milk, warmed

½ cup (2 oz/60 g) shredded mozzarella cheese

1 large egg, beaten

Preheat oven to 400°F (200°C). Spray a 24-cup mini muffin pan with cooking spray.

Bring a saucepan filled with water to a boil over high heat. Add the pasta, reduce heat to medium, and cook until al dente, about 10 minutes or according to package directions. Using a slotted spoon, transfer the pasta to a colander to drain, then roughly chop the pasta. Return the water to a boil and add the broccoli and carrot. After 4 minutes, add the peas. Simmer until the vegetables are tender, about 6 minutes total. Drain the vegetables in the colander.

In the same saucepan over medium heat, melt the butter. Add the garlic, if using, and the flour and whisk until combined. Slowly add the milk while whisking constantly until smooth. Continuing to whisk, slowly add the cheese until smooth. The sauce will be thick. Switch to a spoon and stir in the pasta and vegetables, then stir in the egg until well combined.

Spoon the pasta mixture into about 16 of the prepared muffin cups, dividing it evenly and filling the cups. Bake until crisp and browned around the edges and bubbling, about 15 minutes. Allow to cool in the pan for about 10 minutes before removing (use a small knife to help dislodge them if necessary).

STORE IT Refrigerate in an airtight container for up to 3 days, or seal in a zippered plastic bag and freeze for up to 3 months.

PACK IT Thaw 2 or 3 pasta bites, if necessary, then pack in a small airtight container. If you are on the go for more than 1 hour, place in a small bag with a travel ice pack.

mushroom penne bites

If garlicky mushrooms are a brand new flavor for your little one, this is a great way to introduce it—with nutritious whole-wheat pasta and creamy, nutty cheese. You can leave these pasta bites whole or cut them up into smaller bites. Either way, they are great for packing into an airtight container for nourishment on the go.

MAKES ABOUT 16 BITES

Olive oil cooking spray

Scant 1 cup (3 oz/90g) whole-wheat penne or other pasta shape

1 tablespoon unsalted butter

¼ teaspoon minced garlic (optional)

1 cup (3 oz/90 g) finely chopped button or cremini mushrooms

Salt

2 teaspoons all-purpose flour

⅓ cup (3 fl oz/80 ml) plus 1 tablespoon whole milk, warmed

½ cup (2 oz/60 g) shredded Gruyère or fontina cheese

1 large egg, beaten

Preheat the oven to 375°F (190°C). Spray a 24-cup mini muffin pan with cooking spray.

Bring a saucepan filled with water to a boil over high heat. Add the pasta, reduce the heat to medium, and cook until al dente, about 12 minutes or according to package directions. Drain the pasta, then roughly chop it and set aside.

In the same saucepan over medium heat, melt the butter. Add the garlic, if using, the mushrooms, and a pinch of salt and sauté until the mushrooms are tender, about 4 minutes. Add the flour and whisk until combined. Slowly add the milk while whisking constantly until smooth. Switch to a spoon and slowly add the cheese, stirring constantly. The mixture will be thick. Stir in the pasta, then stir in the egg until well combined.

Spoon the pasta mixture into about 16 of the prepared muffin cups, dividing it evenly and filling the cups. Bake until crisp and browned around the edges and bubbling, about 15 minutes. Allow to cool in the pan for about 10 minutes before removing (use a small knife to help dislodge them if necessary).

STORE IT Refrigerate in an airtight container for up to 3 days, or seal in a zippered plastic bag and freeze for up to 3 months.

PACK IT Thaw 2 or 3 penne bites, if necessary, then pack in a small airtight container. If you are on the go for more than 1 hour, place in a small bag with a travel ice pack.

spinach & cheese frittata bites

Frittatas are great because you can put almost anything into them and make them delicious. This recipe is just a starting point. Try any kind of shredded or chopped cooked vegetables, chopped meat or poultry, and whatever melting cheese you might have on hand. It's the best, most tasty way you can use up what you have in the fridge.

MAKES ABOUT 12 BITES

Olive oil cooking spray

1 teaspoon olive oil

2 packed cups (3 oz/90 g) fresh baby spinach

3 large eggs, lightly beaten

1 tablespoon whole milk

¼ teaspoon minced fresh oregano

Salt and freshly ground pepper

2 tablespoons crumbled fresh goat cheese

Preheat oven to 350°F (180°C). Spray a 24-cup mini muffin pan with cooking spray.

In a frying pan over medium heat, warm the oil. Add the spinach and sauté until it releases its liquid, about 2 minutes. Drain, squeezing to remove the liquid, then chop finely.

In a bowl, whisk together the eggs, milk, oregano, a pinch each of salt and pepper, and the cooked spinach. Divide the mixture evenly among about 12 of the prepared cups; they should be almost full. Divide the cheese evenly among the filled cups, scattering it on top.

Bake the mini frittatas until the centers are set and the edges are browned and pulling away from the pan sides, about 15 minutes. If you like, turn on the broiler during the last minute of cooking to brown the tops. Transfer to a wire rack and let cool in the pan for 5 minutes. Run a small knife around the inside edge of each muffin cup to release the mini frittatas, then turn out onto the rack. Let cool.

STORE IT Refrigerate in an airtight container for up to 3 days, or seal in a zippered plastic bag and freeze for up to 3 months.

PACK IT Thaw 2 or 3 frittata bites, if necessary, then pack in a small airtight container. If you are on the go for more than 1 hour, place in a small bag with a travel ice pack.

more frittata bites

These sunny yellow protein-packed nuggets can be just about any flavor you want them to be. Use any combination of vegetable and meat and/or cheese that appeals to you and your toddler. Here are four ideas to get you started. For each recipe, preheat the oven to 350°F (180°C). Spray a 24-cup mini muffin pan with cooking spray. Follow the instructions to make the frittata bites, then bake until set and golden brown, about 15 minutes. Transfer to a wire rack and let cool for 5 minutes, then release the mini frittatas onto the rack and let cool.

mexican chicken & jack

In a bowl, whisk together 3 large eggs, 1 tablespoon milk, ¼ cup (1½ oz/45 g) finely chopped cooked chicken, ¼ teaspoon minced fresh oregano, ¼ teaspoon mild chili powder, and a pinch each of salt and pepper. Divide the mixture among about 12 of the cups, then sprinkle 2 tablespoons shredded jack cheese on top, dividing it evenly. Bake and cool according to the directions above.

ham, tomato & swiss

In a bowl, whisk together 3 large eggs, 1 tablespoon milk, ¼ cup (1½ oz/45 g) finely chopped Black Forest ham, 1 tablespoon finely chopped sun-dried tomato (optional), and a pinch each of salt and pepper. Divide the mixture among about 12 of the cups, then sprinkle 2 tablespoons shredded Swiss cheese on top, dividing it evenly. Bake and cool according to the directions above.

asparagus & mozzarella

In a bowl, whisk together 3 large eggs, 1 tablespoon milk, ¼ cup (1½ oz/45 g) finely chopped cooked asparagus, and a pinch each of salt and pepper. Divide the mixture among the cups, then sprinkle 2 tablespoons shredded mozzarella cheese on top, dividing it evenly among about 12 of the cups. Bake and cool according to the directions above.

cherry tomato & feta

In a bowl, whisk together 3 large eggs, 1 tablespoon milk, ¼ cup (1½ oz/45 g) finely chopped cherry tomatoes, ½ teaspoon minced fresh thyme, and a pinch each of salt and pepper. Divide the mixture among about 12 of the cups, then sprinkle 2 tablespoons crumbled feta cheese on top, dividing it evenly. Bake and cool according to the directions above.

frittata pasta bites

Adding pasta to your frittata makes it all the more appealing to little ones, especially if they like pasta. This recipe is also a good way to use up that small portion of leftover pasta you have on hand from last night's dinner. You can even use spaghetti or linguine: just chop it up into small bits before adding it to the mix.

MAKES ABOUT 12 FRITTATA BITES

Olive oil cooking spray

½ cup (2 oz/60 g) cooked whole-wheat elbow macaroni or orzo (page 61)

1 teaspoon olive oil

2 large eggs, lightly beaten

2 teaspoons whole milk

¼ cup (1 oz/30 g) grated Parmesan cheese

1 teaspoon finely chopped fresh basil

Preheat the oven to 350°F (180°). Spray a 24-cup mini muffin pan with cooking spray.

Toss the cooked pasta with the oil, then divide it evenly among about 12 of the prepared muffin cups. In a bowl, whisk together the eggs, milk, cheese, and basil. Divide the mixture evenly among the filled cups.

Bake the mini frittatas until the centers are set and the edges are browned and pulling away from the pan sides, about 15 minutes. If you like, turn on the broiler during the last minute of cooking to brown the tops. Transfer to a wire rack and let cool for 5 minutes. Run a small knife around the inside edge of each muffin cup to release the mini frittatas, then turn out onto the rack. Let cool.

STORE IT Refrigerate in an airtight container for up to 3 days, or seal in a zippered plastic bag and freeze for up to 3 months.

PACK IT Thaw 2 or 3 frittata bites, if necessary, then pack in a small airtight container. If you are on the go for more than 1 hour, place in a small bag with a travel ice pack.

great grains frittata bites

Whole grains, like bulgur, farro, or wheat berries, or pseudo-grains, like quinoa, add heft, fiber, and nutrients to these protein-rich frittata bites. They also carry complex carbohydrates, which give my little girl enough energy to keep her happy all afternoon. Make sure the grains are fully cooked for easy digestion.

MAKES ABOUT 12 FRITTATA BITES

Olive oil cooking spray

⅓ cup (2½ oz/75 g) cooked whole grains, such as barley (page 44) or quinoa (page 45)

1 teaspoon olive oil

3 large eggs, lightly beaten

2 teaspoons whole milk

1 tablespoon finely chopped jarred roasted red bell pepper

1 teaspoon finely chopped fresh basil

2 tablespoons shredded Cheddar cheese

Salt and freshly ground pepper

Preheat the oven to 350°F (180°). Spray a 24-cup mini muffin pan with cooking spray. Toss the cooked grains with oil.

In a bowl, whisk together the eggs, milk, grains, roasted pepper, and basil. Divide the mixture evenly among about 12 of the prepared muffin cups; they should be almost full. Top each with a little cheese, dividing it evenly.

Bake the mini frittatas until the centers are set and the edges are browned and pulling away from the pan sides, about 15 minutes. If you like, turn on the broiler during the last minute of cooking to brown the tops. Transfer to a wire rack and let cool for 5 minutes. Run a knife around the inside edge of each muffin cup to release the mini frittatas, then turn out onto the rack. Let cool.

STORE IT Refrigerate in an airtight container for up to 3 days, or seal in a zippered plastic bag and freeze for up to 3 months.

PACK IT Thaw 2 or 3 frittata bites, if necessary, then pack in a small airtight container. If you are on the go for more than 1 hour, place in a small bag with a travel ice pack.

spanish potato tortilla bites

A Spanish tortilla is a frittata-like "cake" made with sliced potatoes and onions that are simmered in olive oil, mixed with eggs, and then fried in a pan. This simpler, healthier version adds ham, egg, and cheese to a sautéed potato and onion mixture, which is then baked in a mini muffin pan. These tasty bites never last long in our refrigerator.

MAKES ABOUT 12 BITES

Olive oil cooking spray

2 large eggs, beaten

2 teaspoons whole milk

1 teaspoon olive oil

¼ yellow onion, finely chopped

½ cup (2½ oz/75 g) finely diced cooked, peeled potato

2 tablespoons finely chopped Black Forest ham (optional)

2 tablespoons shredded Monterey jack cheese

Preheat the oven to 375°F (190°C). Spray a 24-cup mini muffin pan with cooking spray.

In a bowl, whisk together the eggs and milk. Set aside. In a frying pan over medium heat, warm the oil. Add the onion and sauté until lightly browned and very tender, about 5 minutes. Add the potato and the ham, if using, and sauté until warmed through, about 2 minutes.

Add the potato mixture to the egg mixture and stir to mix. Divide the mixture evenly among about 12 of the prepared muffin cups; they should be almost full. Top with the cheese, dividing it evenly.

Bake the mini tortillas until the centers are set and the edges are browned and pulling away from the pan sides, about 15 minutes. If you like, turn on the broiler during the last minute of cooking to brown the tops. Transfer to a wire rack and let cool for 5 minutes. Run a knife around the inside edge of each muffin cup to release the mini tortillas, then turn out onto the rack. Let cool.

STORE IT Refrigerate in an airtight container for up to 3 days, or seal in a zippered plastic bag and freeze for up to 3 months.

PACK IT Thaw 2 or 3 tortilla bites, if necessary, then pack in a small airtight container. If you are on the go for more than 1 hour, place in a small bag with a travel ice pack.

mushroom bread tartlets

Whole-wheat bread makes a surprising crust for these custardy mushroom and green onion tartlets. The bread crisps up nicely, making these tartlets easy to transport and an easy to eat meal-in-one package. If you opt for multigrain bread, look for a loaf with a whole-wheat flour base and a good mix of grains, such as oats, millet, cracked wheat, cornmeal, and flax.

MAKES 6 TARTLETS

Olive oil cooking spray

6 slices whole-wheat or multigrain bread

1 tablespoon unsalted butter, melted

2½ oz (75 g) cremini or button mushrooms (about 5), finely chopped

1 green onion, white and tender green parts, finely chopped

2 tablespoons cream cheese, at room temperature

2 large eggs, lightly beaten

2 tablespoons shredded Cheddar or mozzarella cheese

Preheat the oven to 350°F (180°C). Spray a 12-cup standard muffin pan with cooking spray.

Using a 3¼-inch (8-cm) biscuit cutter, cut out a round from each bread slice. Flatten the bread rounds with your hand, then brush both sides of each round with half of the butter, dividing it evenly. Press each round into 6 of the prepared muffin cups.

In a small saucepan over medium heat, warm the remaining butter. Add the mushrooms and green onion and sauté until tender, about 3 minutes. Transfer to a bowl and stir in the cream cheese. Add the eggs and beat together with a fork until smooth. Divide the mixture among the lined muffin cups. The cups will be very full but the bread will soak up some of the egg. Top each cup with an equal amount of the cheese.

Bake until the bread is golden and toasted, the cheese is bubbling, and the egg is cooked through, about 13 minutes. Remove from the pan and transfer to a wire rack. Use a small knife to help dislodge them if necessary. Let cool.

STORE IT Refrigerate in an airtight container for up to 1 day, or seal in a zippered plastic bag and freeze for up to 3 months.

PACK IT Thaw 1 tartlet, if necessary, then pack in a small airtight container. If you are on the go for more than 1 hour, place in a small bag with a travel ice pack.

ham & veggie mini quiches

Miniature quiches may seem like a lot of work, but you can cut out the dough and line the muffin cups whenever you have a moment, then just put the pan in the refrigerator for up to 1 day or in the freezer for up to 3 days until you have time to make the filling. If the dough is frozen, bring it to cool room temperature before filling and baking.

MAKES ABOUT 14 MINI QUICHES

Olive oil cooking spray

1 sheet frozen all-butter pie dough, about 11 inches (28 cm) square, thawed

2 large eggs

2 tablespoons whole milk

¼ cup (1 oz/30 g) finely chopped cooked broccoli or spinach (page 35)

2 tablespoons finely chopped Black Forest ham

¼ cup (1 oz/30 g) finely grated Cheddar cheese

Spray a 24-cup mini muffin pan with cooking spray. Place the dough on a lightly floured work surface and roll out until it is about ⅛ inch (3 mm) thick, if necessary. Using a 2½-inch (6-cm) round biscuit cutter, cut out as many rounds as possible. You should get about 14 rounds. (If necessary, gather up the scraps, roll out ⅛ inch thick, and cut out additional rounds.) Make sure the dough stays very cold as you work with it; place it in the refrigerator at any time if it gets too warm. Press the rounds into the prepared cups. The edges of the dough should be flush with the rim of each cup. Refrigerate while you prepare the filling.

Preheat the oven to 400°F (200°C). In a large measuring pitcher, whisk together the eggs and milk. Divide the broccoli and ham evenly among the lined cups, and then pour the egg mixture into the cups, leaving a little space at the top and dividing it evenly. (If you have leftover filling, use it to fill the unlined cups for quick frittatas.) Top each cup with an equal amount of the cheese.

Bake until the mini quiches are puffy and golden brown, about 20 minutes. Let cool in the pan on a wire rack for about 10 minutes. Run a small knife around the inside edge of each cup and carefully lift out the quiches.

STORE IT Refrigerate in an airtight container for up to 3 days, or seal in a zippered plastic bag and freeze for up to 3 months.

PACK IT Thaw 2 or 3 mini quiches, if necessary, then pack in a small airtight container. If you are on the go for more than 1 hour, place in a small bag with a travel ice pack.

mini salmon cakes

These bite-sized salmon cakes are a great way to introduce your toddler to fish. And salmon is chock-full of healthy omega-3 fatty acids, which are essential to a healthful diet. To make eating these cakes even more fun, bring along some plain whole-milk yogurt for your toddler to use for dipping.

MAKES ABOUT 12 MINI CAKES

Olive oil cooking spray

About ½ lb (250 g) skinless salmon fillet, cut into 4 chunks

1 large egg, lightly beaten

2 tablespoons fine dried bread crumbs

2 teaspoons mayonnaise

¼ teaspoon minced fresh dill (optional)

1 teaspoon fresh lemon juice

Kosher salt

Preheat the oven to 375°F (190°C). Spray a 24-cup mini muffin pan with cooking spray.

Wrap the salmon chunks in aluminum foil and bake in the oven until opaque, about 10 minutes. Remove from the foil and let cool for about 10 minutes. Using a fork, flake the salmon into small pieces, discarding any errant bones.

In a bowl, stir together the egg, bread crumbs, mayonnaise, dill (if using), lemon juice, and a pinch of salt. Stir in the salmon. Divide the salmon mixture evenly among about 12 of the prepared muffin cups.

Bake the cakes until lightly browned and set, about 13 minutes. Let cool in the pan on a wire rack for about 10 minutes. Run a small knife around the inside edge of each cup and carefully lift out the cakes. Let cool on the rack.

NOTE If allergies run in your family, you may wish to delay introducing fish; consult your pediatrician.

STORE IT Refrigerate in an airtight container for up to 1 day, or seal in a zippered plastic bag and freeze for up to 3 months.

PACK IT Thaw 2 or 3 salmon cakes, if necessary, then pack in a small airtight container. Place in a small bag with a travel ice pack.

mini turkey meat loaves

You can make these little meat loaves even more nourishing by adding shredded zucchini or chopped sautéed spinach. If you and your toddler are on the go, these mini loaves provide the perfect hit of protein when hunger strikes. Plus, they travel easily along with roasted or steamed vegetables and cucumber-yogurt dip (page 146) for a complete meal.

MAKES ABOUT 24 MINI MEAT LOAVES

Olive oil cooking spray

½ cup (1 oz/30 g) fresh or fine dried bread crumbs

¼ cup (2 fl oz/60 ml) whole milk

1 tablespoon tomato paste

½ teaspoon kosher salt

1 large egg, lightly beaten

⅓ cup (1½ oz/45 g) shredded zucchini

1 lb (500 g) ground dark-meat turkey

Preheat the oven to 425°F (220°C). Spray a rimmed baking sheet with cooking spray.

In a bowl, combine the bread crumbs and milk and let stand for about 5 minutes. Add the tomato paste, salt, egg, and zucchini and stir to mix well. Add the turkey and mix gently just until blended. Drop tablespoonfuls of the meat mixture onto the prepared baking sheet, spacing them evenly.

Bake until the mini meat loaves are browned and cooked through, about 13 minutes. Let cool, then cut into halves, quarters, or other sizes that your toddler can handle.

STORE IT Refrigerate in an airtight container for up to 1 day, or seal in a zippered plastic bag and freeze for up to 3 months.

PACK IT Thaw 2 or 3 mini meat loaves, if necessary, then pack in a small airtight container. Place in a small bag with a travel ice pack.

meatballs

These are the meatballs I grew up eating. The addition of cinnamon may seem strange, but trust me, it makes these bite-sized balls taste wonderful. Serve these on their own, slice them and stuff them into a mini whole-wheat pita bread with plain whole-milk yogurt and chopped cherry tomatoes, or turn them into a mini meatball sandwich (page 131).

MAKES ABOUT 30 MINI MEATBALLS

Olive oil cooking spray

½ cup (1 oz/30 g) fresh or fine dried bread crumbs

¼ cup (2 fl oz/60 ml) whole milk

1 tablespoon minced yellow onion (optional)

½ teaspoon ground cumin

' ½ teaspoon cinnamon

¼ teaspoon kosher salt

1 large egg, lightly beaten

1 lb (500 g) ground beef or a mixture of ground beef and ground pork

Preheat the oven to 425°F (220°C). Spray a large rimmed baking sheet with cooking spray.

In a bowl, combine the bread crumbs and milk and let stand for about 5 minutes. Add the onion, cumin, cinnamon, and salt and stir. Add the egg and beef and gently mix the ingredients just until blended. Scoop up heaping tablespoonfuls of the meat mixture, roll into mini meatballs, and set on the prepared baking sheet, spacing them evenly.

Bake until the meatballs are browned and cooked through, about 15 minutes. Let cool, then cut into halves, quarters, or other sizes that your toddler can handle.

STORE IT Refrigerate in an airtight container for up to 1 day, or seal in a zippered plastic bag and freeze for up to 3 months.

PACK IT Thaw 2 or 3 meatballs, if necessary, then pack in a small airtight container. Place in a small bag with a travel ice pack.

curried lentil-rice cakes

The curry powder is what sets these lentil and brown rice cakes apart. But if it's too much spice for your little one, you can leave it out. Make sure to select a mild curry powder, unless you know your toddler likes spicy food (mine does). Lentils are a good source of iron, manganese, and folate, and lentils and brown rice together pack plenty of protein.

MAKES 12 MINI CAKES

¼ cup (2 oz/60 g) French or other lentils

Olive oil cooking spray

⅓ cup (2 oz/60 g) cooked brown rice

2 tablespoons fine dried bread crumbs

½ teaspoon mild yellow curry powder

Kosher salt

1 large egg, lightly beaten

Plain whole-milk yogurt for serving

In a saucepan, combine the lentils and 2 cups (16 fl oz/500 ml) water. Bring to a boil over high heat, reduce the heat to medium-low, and simmer until tender but not mushy, about 20 minutes. Drain. You should have about ¾ cup (4½ oz/140 g) cooked lentils.

Preheat the oven to 400°F (200°C). Spray a 24-cup mini muffin pan with cooking spray.

In a bowl, stir together the lentils, rice, bread crumbs, curry powder, and a pinch of salt. Stir in the egg. Divide the lentil mixture evenly among about 12 of the prepared muffin cups.

Bake until the cakes are lightly browned and set, about 13 minutes. Let cool in the pan on a wire rack for about 10 minutes. Run a small knife around the inside edge of each cup and carefully lift out the cakes. Let cool on the rack. Serve the cakes with the yogurt for dipping.

STORE IT Refrigerate in an airtight container for up to 3 days, or seal in a zippered plastic bag and freeze for up to 3 months.

PACK IT Thaw 2 or 3 lentil cakes, if necessary, then pack in a small airtight container. Pack a separate small airtight container with yogurt. If you are on the go for more than 1 hour, place both containers in a small bag with a travel ice pack.

baked mini arancini

In southern Italy, arancini, stuffed rice balls coated with bread crumbs and deep-fried, are popular. My toddler-friendly baked version calls for brown rice, spinach, and mozzarella. These balls are a favorite of everyone in our house, both toddler and adult. Short-grain brown rice cooks to a softer texture than long grain, making it a better choice for this dish.

MAKES ABOUT 16 MINI ARANCINI

Olive oil cooking spray

¼ cup (1½ oz/45 g) all-purpose flour

1 large egg, lightly beaten

¼ cup (1 oz/30 g) fine dried bread crumbs

1 cup (5 oz/155 g) cooled cooked brown rice, preferably short grain

⅓ cup (1½ oz/45 g) shredded mozzarella cheese

¼ cup (2 oz/60 g) finely chopped cooked spinach (page 35)

Purchased tomato sauce for serving (optional)

Preheat the oven to 400°F (200°C). Spray a rimmed baking sheet with cooking spray.

Put the flour in one bowl, the egg in a second bowl, and the bread crumbs in a third bowl.

In another bowl, stir together the rice, mozzarella, and spinach, mixing well. Roll about 1 heaping tablespoon of the rice mixture between your palms into a ball. Roll the ball in the flour, then in the egg, and finally, in the bread crumbs, shaking off any excess with each step. Place the coated ball on the prepared baking sheet. Repeat with the remaining rice mixture; you should get about 14 balls. Rinse your hands as you go so they don't get too coated.

Bake the balls for 8 minutes, then turn them over. if some of the cheese leaks out, just tuck it back around the balls. Continue to bake until the balls are crisp and golden brown, about 8 minutes more. Let cool before serving. Serve the arancini with the tomato sauce for dipping, if desired.

STORE IT Refrigerate in an airtight container for up to 3 days, or seal in a zippered plastic bag and freeze for up to 3 months.

PACK IT Thaw 2 or 3 arancini, if necessary, then pack in a small airtight container. Pack a separate small airtight container with sauce.
If you are on the go for more than 1 hour, place both containers in a small bag with a travel ice pack.

master muffin dry mix

This clever formula is great to have on hand to make mini muffins for your little one at nearly a moment's notice. It takes just minutes to put together the mix (you can do it while your child is napping) and makes baking easy. Simply add wet ingredients and the desired flavorings, according to your recipe of choice, and bake.

In a bowl, whisk together 1½ cups (7½ oz/235 g) all-purpose flour; 2 cups (10 oz/315 g) white-whole-wheat or whole-wheat flour; ¾ cup (2 oz/60 g) wheat bran; 4 teaspoons baking powder; 1 teaspoon baking soda; ½ teaspoon kosher salt; and ¾ cup (6 oz/185 g) firmly packed golden brown sugar until well blended. Store in a zippered plastic freezer bag in the refrigerator for up to 1 month.

Follow the recipes on pages 89 and 90 to make muffins. Makes 5 cups (about 30 oz/940 g) mix (enough for 5 batches of muffins).

fruit mini muffins

Healthful and tasty, these muffins will disappear quickly. Although blueberry, apple, or banana tends to win over little hearts right away, you can also try chopped ripe peaches or mangoes or raspberries. Always keep a batch of the muffin mix on hand and you'll be able to whip up these fruit-laced muffins whenever you have a little time in your day.

MAKES ABOUT 16 MINI MUFFINS

Canola oil cooking spray (optional)

1 large egg, lightly beaten

2 tablespoons canola oil

¼ cup (2 oz/60 g) plain whole-milk Greek yogurt

½ teaspoon pure vanilla extract

For banana muffins ⅛ teaspoon grated nutmeg, ¼ teaspoon ground cinnamon, ½ cup (4 oz/125 g) mashed banana

For blueberry muffins ½ teaspoon grated orange zest, ½ cup (2 oz/60 g) fresh or frozen blueberries

For apple muffins ½ teaspoon ground cinnamon, ½ cup (1½ oz/45 g) shredded peeled apple

1 cup (5 oz/155 g) Master Muffin Mix (page 87), or see note

Preheat the oven to 400°F (200°C). Spray a 24-cup mini muffin pan with cooking spray or line with paper liners.

In a bowl, beat together the egg, oil, yogurt, and vanilla. Stir in the spices and fruit of your choice. (If using the apple, pat it dry with paper towels before adding it to the other ingredients.) Add the muffin mix and stir just until evenly moistened. The batter will be thick.

Spoon the batter into the prepared muffin cups, dividing it evenly among about 16 cups and filling the cups. Bake until the muffins are golden brown and a toothpick inserted into the center of a muffin comes out clean, about 13 minutes. Let the muffins cool in the pan on a wire rack for about 5 minutes, then transfer to the wire rack to cool.

NOTE If you don't have the muffin mix on hand, in a bowl, stir together ⅓ cup (1½ oz/45 g) all-purpose flour, ⅓ cup (1½ oz/45 g) white-whole-wheat or whole-wheat flour, 2 tablespoons wheat bran, 1 teaspoon baking powder, ¼ teaspoon baking soda, ¼ teaspoon kosher salt, and 2 tablespoons packed golden brown sugar, mixing well. Proceed with the recipe.

STORE IT Refrigerate in an airtight container for up to 3 days, or seal in a zippered plastic bag and freeze for up to 3 months.

PACK IT Thaw 2 or 3 mini muffins, if necessary, then pack in a small airtight container.

veggie spice muffins

These bite-sized muffins are loaded with healthful ingredients—whole-wheat flour, wheat bran, shredded carrot or zucchini, yogurt, applesauce—to fuel your toddler's afternoon playtime. Here, I've added just enough cinnamon and ginger to the batter to delight your little one's palate without overwhelming it.

MAKES ABOUT 16 MINI MUFFINS

Canola oil cooking spray (optional)

½ cup (2½ oz/75 g) shredded carrot or zucchini

1 large egg, lightly beaten

2 tablespoons canola oil

¼ cup (2 oz/60 g) plain whole-milk Greek yogurt

¼ cup (2¼ oz/70 g) unsweetened applesauce

½ teaspoon pure vanilla extract

¼ teaspoon ground cinnamon

¼ teaspoon ground ginger

1 cup (5 oz/155 g) Master Muffin Mix (page 87), or see note

Preheat the oven to 400°F (200°C). Spray a 24-cup mini muffin pan with cooking spray or line with paper liners. Pat the carrot or zucchini dry with paper towels.

In a bowl, beat together the egg, oil, yogurt, applesauce, vanilla, spices, and carrot or zucchini. Add the muffin mix and stir just until evenly moistened. The batter will be thick.

Spoon the batter into the prepared muffin cups, dividing it evenly among about 16 cups and filling the cups. Bake until the muffins are golden brown and a toothpick inserted into the center of a muffin comes out clean, about 13 minutes. Let the muffins cool in the pan on a wire rack for about 5 minutes, then transfer to the wire rack to cool.

NOTE If you don't have the muffin mix on hand, in a bowl, stir together ⅓ cup (1½ oz/45 g) all-purpose flour, ⅓ cup (1½ oz/45 g) white-whole-wheat or whole-wheat flour, 2 tablespoons wheat bran, 1 teaspoon baking powder, ¼ teaspoon baking soda, ¼ teaspoon kosher salt, and 2 tablespoons packed golden brown sugar, mixing well. Proceed with the recipe.

STORE IT Refrigerate in an airtight container for up to 3 days, or seal in a zippered plastic bag and freeze for up to 3 months.

PACK IT Thaw 2 or 3 mini muffins, if necessary, then pack in a small airtight container.

oatmeal-raisin muffins

Here is the classic oatmeal-raisin cookie reinterpreted as a wholesome mini muffin. Made from whole-wheat flour, rolled oats, and oat bran, these muffins are packed with the complex carbohydrates needed for energy. If your toddler is not yet eating whole raisins, make sure you finely chop the raisins so they don't pose a choking risk.

MAKES ABOUT 16 MINI MUFFINS

Canola oil cooking spray (optional)

½ cup (2½ oz/75 g) white-whole-wheat or whole-wheat flour

⅓ cup (1 oz/30 g) old-fashioned rolled oats

2 tablespoons oat bran

1 teaspoon baking powder

¼ teaspoon *each baking soda and kosher salt*

2 tablespoons packed golden brown sugar

1 large egg, lightly beaten

2 tablespoons canola oil

¼ cup (2 oz/60 g) plain whole-milk Greek yogurt

¼ cup (2¼ oz/70 g) unsweetened applesauce

½ teaspoon pure vanilla extract

½ teaspoon ground cinnamon

2 tablespoons raisins, chopped

Preheat the oven to 400°F (200°C). Spray a 24-cup mini muffin pan with cooking spray or line with paper liners.

In a bowl, stir together the flour, oats, oat bran, baking powder, baking soda, salt, and sugar. In another bowl, beat together the egg, oil, yogurt, applesauce, vanilla, cinnamon, and raisins. Add the dry ingredients to the egg mixture and stir just until evenly moistened.

Spoon the batter into the prepared muffin cups, dividing it evenly among about 16 cups and filling the cups. Bake until the muffins are golden brown and a toothpick inserted into the center of a muffin comes out clean, about 13 minutes. Let the muffins cool in the pan on a wire rack for about 5 minutes, then transfer to the wire rack to cool.

STORE IT Refrigerate in an airtight container for up to 3 days, or seal in a zippered plastic bag and freeze for up to 3 months.

PACK IT Thaw 2 or 3 mini muffins, if necessary, then pack in a small airtight container.

multigrain cereal muffins

Raisin bran or another bran cereal ensures these simple muffins have great texture. Pack these up for breakfast on the go or for an afternoon snack when you and your toddler are out running errands. Add a sippy cup of milk and it's almost like your child is eating a wholesome bowl of cereal.

MAKES ABOUT 16 MINI MUFFINS

Canola oil cooking spray

½ cup (1 oz/30 g) raisin bran cereal

¼ cup (2 fl oz/60 ml) whole milk

1 large egg, lightly beaten

2 tablespoons canola oil

⅓ cup (3 oz/90 g) unsweetened applesauce

⅓ cup (2 oz/60 g) whole-wheat flour

1 teaspoon baking powder

¼ teaspoon baking soda

¼ teaspoon kosher salt

2 tablespoons packed golden brown sugar

Preheat the oven to 400°F (200°C). Spray a 24-cup mini muffin pan with cooking spray or line with paper liners.

In a bowl, stir together the cereal and milk. Let stand for 10 minutes to soften, then stir in the egg, oil, and applesauce. In another bowl, stir together the flour, baking powder, baking soda, salt, and sugar. Add the dry ingredients to the bran mixture and stir just until evenly moistened. The batter will be thick.

Spoon the batter into the prepared muffin cups, dividing it evenly among about 16 cups and filling the cups. Bake until the muffins are golden brown and a toothpick inserted into the center of a muffin comes out clean, about 13 minutes. Let the muffins cool in the pan on a wire rack for about 5 minutes, then transfer to the wire rack to cool.

STORE IT Refrigerate in an airtight container for up to 3 days, or seal in a zippered plastic bag and freeze for up to 3 months.

PACK IT Thaw 2 or 3 mini muffins, if necessary, then pack in a small airtight container.

mini cheese biscuits

These fluffy biscuits are made in a mini muffin pan, but you can also just drop
tablespoonfuls onto a parchment paper–lined baking sheet and bake them as you
would regular biscuits. I like using a mix of whole-wheat and white flours,
but you can use all white flour if you want to make a more traditional biscuit.

MAKES ABOUT 12 MINI BISCUITS

**Canola oil cooking spray
(optional)**

**⅓ cup (2 oz/60 g)
all-purpose flour**

**⅓ cup (2 oz/60 g) white-
whole-wheat or
whole-wheat flour**

1 teaspoon baking powder

¼ teaspoon baking soda

¼ teaspoon kosher salt

**⅓ cup (2½ oz/75 g)
buttermilk or yogurt**

**2 tablespoons unsalted
butter, melted**

**⅓ cup (1½ oz/45 g)
shredded Cheddar cheese**

Preheat the oven to 400°F (200°C). Spray a 24-cup mini muffin pan with
cooking spray or line with paper liners.

In a bowl, stir together the flours, baking powder, baking soda, and salt.
Stir in the buttermilk, butter, and cheese just until all of the ingredients
are evenly moistened. The dough will be stiff.

Spoon the dough into the prepared muffin cups, dividing it evenly
among about 12 cups and filling the cups. Bake until the biscuits are
golden brown and a toothpick inserted into the center of a biscuit
comes out clean, 10–12 minutes. Let the biscuits cool in the pan on
a wire rack for about 5 minutes, then transfer to the wire rack to cool.

STORE IT Refrigerate in an airtight container for up to 3 days, or seal
in a zippered plastic bag and freeze for up to 3 months.

PACK IT Thaw 2 or 3 mini biscuits, if necessary, then pack in a small
airtight container.

savory mini corn muffins

Studded with sweet corn kernels and savory bits of Cheddar cheese, these bite-sized cornbread muffins are a great on-the-go snack or a good accompaniment to meat loaves (page 81) or meatballs (page 82) at the dinner table. I like to add a small amount of sugar to the batter, but you can leave it out, if you like.

MAKES ABOUT 16 MINI MUFFINS

Canola oil cooking spray (optional)

⅓ cup (2½ oz/75 g) cornmeal

⅓ cup (2 oz/60 g) white-whole-wheat or whole-wheat flour

1 teaspoon baking powder

¼ teaspoon baking soda

⅛ teaspoon kosher salt

1 teaspoon packed golden brown sugar

1 large egg, lightly beaten

2 tablespoons canola oil

¼ cup (2 oz/60 g) plain whole-milk Greek yogurt

⅓ cup (1½ oz/45 g) shredded Cheddar cheese

¼ cup (1½ oz/45 g) fresh or frozen corn kernels

Preheat the oven to 400°F (200°C). Spray a 24-cup mini muffin pan with cooking spray or line with paper liners.

In a bowl, stir together the cornmeal, flour, baking powder, baking soda, salt, and sugar. In another bowl, beat together the egg, oil, and yogurt. Stir in the cheese and corn kernels. Add the dry ingredients to the egg mixture and stir just until evenly moistened. The batter will be thick.

Spoon the batter into the prepared muffin cups, dividing it evenly among about 16 cups and filling the cups. Bake until the muffins are golden brown and a toothpick inserted into the center of a muffin comes out clean, about 13 minutes. Let the muffins cool in the pan on a wire rack for about 5 minutes, then transfer to the wire rack to cool.

STORE IT Refrigerate in an airtight container for up to 3 days, or seal in a zippered plastic bag and freeze for up to 3 months.

PACK IT Thaw 2 or 3 mini muffins, if necessary, then pack in a small airtight container.

g-f blueberry-almond muffins

It's always a good idea to have a gluten-free muffin in your repertoire in case your toddler or even your toddler's friends can't eat baked goods that contain gluten. But eating these yummy gluten-free muffins is definitely no hardship. Indeed, this recipe is well worth making whether you are staying away from gluten or not. Try it with other fruits (page 89) if you like.

MAKES ABOUT 18 MUFFINS

Canola oil cooking spray (optional)

½ cup (1½ oz/60 g) almond meal

½ cup (2¾ oz/80 g) brown or white rice flour

¼ cup (1 oz/30 g) tapioca starch

1 teaspoon baking powder

¼ teaspoon baking soda

¼ teaspoon kosher salt

2 tablespoons packed golden brown sugar

1 large egg, lightly beaten

2 tablespoons canola oil

⅓ cup (2½ oz/75 g) plain whole-milk Greek yogurt

¼ cup (1 oz/30 g) blueberries

Preheat the oven to 400°F (200°C). Spray a 24-cup mini muffin pan with cooking spray or line with paper liners.

In a bowl, stir together the almond meal, rice flour, tapioca starch, baking powder, baking soda, salt, and sugar. In another bowl, beat together the egg, oil, and yogurt. Stir in the blueberries. Add the dry ingredients to the egg mixture and stir just until evenly moistened. The batter will be thick.

Spoon the batter into the prepared muffin cups, dividing it evenly among about 18 cups and filling the cups. Bake until the muffins are golden brown and a toothpick inserted into the center of a muffin comes out clean, about 13 minutes. Let the muffins cool in the pan on a wire rack for about 5 minutes, then transfer to the wire rack to cool.

STORE IT Refrigerate in an airtight container for up to 3 days, or seal in a zippered plastic bag and freeze for up to 3 months.

PACK IT Thaw 2 or 3 mini muffins, if necessary, then pack in a small airtight container.

fruit salad

My daughter loves fruit, and mixing up a few different kinds helps keep mealtime fun. These themed fruit salads pair flavors that go together well, and are also in season at the same time. When I bring along minis, I like to pack a fruit salad for the perfect healthy side dish. Pack the fruit in a separate airtight container, then place it in a plastic bag with a travel ice pack.

tropical fruit salad

Peel and dice ¼ cup (1½ oz/45 g) each mango, papaya, kiwi, and banana. In a bowl, gently toss together the diced fruits. If desired, mix in 2 tablespoons plain whole-milk yogurt, a squeeze of lime juice, and 1 tablespoon toasted shredded coconut.

berry fruit salad

In a bowl, gently toss together ¼ cup (1 oz/30 g) blueberries, ¼ cup (1 oz/30 g) raspberries, and ¼ cup (1 oz/30 g) chopped or sliced strawberries. Add a pinch of finely chopped fresh mint, if you like.

stone fruit salad

In a bowl, gently toss together ¼ cup (1½ oz/45 g) peeled and diced peaches or nectarines, ¼ cup (1½ oz/45 g) diced plums, ¼ cup (1½ oz/45 g) peeled and diced apricots, and ¼ cup (1½ oz/45 g) pitted and chopped cherries.

what's in the fridge fruit salad

In a bowl, gently toss together ¼ cup each (about 1 oz/30 g) of whatever fruits you have on hand, such as diced banana, shredded apple, sliced grapes, or chopped strawberries.

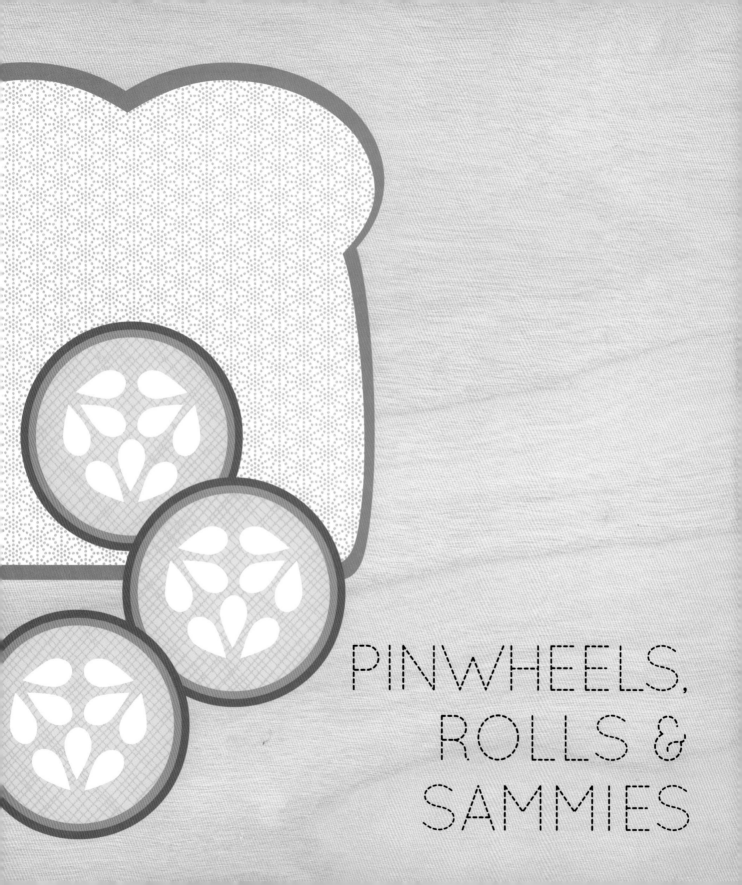

PINWHEELS,
ROLLS &
SAMMIES

fun in all shapes & sizes

Sandwiches are an obvious choice when it comes to food on the go, but eating (and making) the same humdrum versions—peanut butter and jelly, ham and cheese, turkey—can be boring for both parents and toddlers. In this chapter, you'll find not only inspiring new ideas for fillings but also an array of whimsical pinwheels (colorful spirals made from rolled flatbread) and other clever packages that are perfect for feeding kids on the go.

Pinwheels

Pinwheels are fun, versatile, and appealing to nearly every child (and adults, too!). They are made with three primary components: the wrapper, the "glue," and the filling.

The wrapper should be something that is flat and flexible, such as whole-wheat tortillas or lavash. Both are tasty, healthful choices. For the best results, look for tortillas that are 6–8 inches (15–20 cm) in diameter, so the size of the pinwheels won't overwhelm your toddler. You can also use spinach or tomato tortillas to add color, which toddlers love. Lavash comes in spinach and other flavors, as well.

The glue is what you spread on one side of the wrapper to help hold everything together when the wrapper and filling are rolled up. This can be any kind of spread, such as hummus, or a spreadable cheese, like cream cheese or fresh goat cheese. Use the recipes in this chapter as a starting point and then experiment with combinations you know your child will like. Look to the Dips and Dippers chapter for other interesting dips and spreads to use as the "glue" for pinwheels. For example, Black Bean Dip or White Bean Dip (page 141), or Cucumber-

Yogurt Dip (page 146) can be paired with fillings that complement the flavors in the spread.

The filling can be anything your toddler likes to eat, such as shredded or finely chopped vegetables and/or shredded, minced, or thinly sliced meat, poultry, or fish. You'll want to be careful not to stuff the pinwheels with too much filling or they won't hold together once they are sliced.

Rolls

Rolls such as sushi rolls, rice paper rolls (also called fresh spring rolls), and eggplant rolls can be intimidating and more time-intensive to prepare than pinwheels, but they make excellent—and interesting—meals on the go. In fact, they are likely to become recipes that your entire family will enjoy together, rather than meals that only your toddler is eating. Not only are rolls healthful and delicious but there is also real joy in introducing your child to new and interesting food choices in a different package.

Another advantage of sushi rolls and spring rolls is that because their wrappers are generally sturdy, you can usually take them with you anywhere and just slice off pieces as your toddler becomes hungry. They are remarkably versatile, so you can have fun experimenting with different ingredients.

Sammies

I use the term "sammies" as a catchall for all the other types of filling-and-bread combinations that my daughter loves. Sometimes she likes them open-faced; other times she prefers them with a slice of bread on the top and the bottom. Either way, sammies are a favorite when I am super busy and need to put together something quickly before I run out the door with her.

Storing pinwheels, rolls & sammies

Pinwheels and sammies don't store well in the refrigerator for more than about 1 day, and they're not good candidates for freezing. They are best when served the same day you make them. That said, you can do some of the prep work and make some of the fillings in advance to use throughout the week.

Sushi rolls, rice paper rolls, and eggplant rolls can be prepared early in the week and then served over the next 3 to 5 days.

Prep and storage tips

- Shred vegetables in advance and wrap them in plastic wrap to stay fresh.
- Make tuna salad (page 126) or artichoke dip (page 127) early in the week and serve it a few times in the days to come.

Pinwheels, rolls & sammies toolkit

You don't need any special tools or gadgets to make these wholesome snacks.

Spoon for mixing; fork for mashing

Butter knife for spreading

Large, sharp knife for prepping fillings

Serrated knife or other sharp knife for cutting pinwheels

Box grater-shredder for shredding cheese and vegetables

Rimmed baking sheet for cooking vegetables

Frying pan for grilled sammies

Round cake pan for rice paper rolls

Toaster or toaster oven for toasting breads

- Shred the vegetables and prepare the rice or noodles a day before you plan to make sushi or rice paper rolls.
- To bring cream cheese, goat cheese, or Brie to room temperature, remove it from the refrigerator about 30 minutes before you plan to prepare your food.
- Wrap the rolls individually in plastic wrap to make toting them easy.

wrappers & breads

Little hands like little food, so seek out mini versions of breads and wrappers, or cut full-sized ones into fun shapes. Try to purchase whole-wheat, whole-grain, or multigrain products whenever possible.

sliced bread · dinner rolls
English muffins · mini bagels · corn bread
biscuits · mini pitas · lavash
small flour tortillas · small corn tortillas

goat cheese & veggie pinwheels

Creamy, mild goat's milk cheese is the glue that holds these pinwheels—stuffed with lots of crunchy shredded vegetables—together. If your toddler doesn't like the tang of fresh goat cheese, you can swap it for cream cheese. A whole-wheat tortilla has many more nutrients than a white-flour tortilla, plus your toddler will be developing good eating habits early.

MAKES ABOUT 8 PINWHEELS

1 tablespoon shredded carrot

1 tablespoon shredded zucchini

2 tablespoons fresh goat cheese, at room temperature

1 whole-wheat flour tortilla, about 8 inches (20 cm) diameter

Blot the shredded vegetables dry with a paper towel.

Spread the goat cheese evenly over the tortilla, all the way to the edges. Sprinkle the vegetables on top of the cheese, leaving about 1 inch (2.5 cm) uncovered on one side. Starting on the vegetable-covered side, roll up the tortilla into a tight cylinder (the exposed goat cheese will act as a glue to hold the cylinder together).

Trim the ends, and then slice the cylinder crosswise into pinwheels.

PACK & STORE IT Roll the sliced cylinder in plastic wrap or aluminum foil, folding the ends over to keep it secure. Or, arrange pinwheels, one cut side down, in a parchment paper–lined airtight container. Store in the refrigerator until ready to go, up to 1 day.

hummus & veggie pinwheels

MAKES ABOUT 8 PINWHEELS

**1 tablespoon
shredded carrot**

**1 tablespoon finely
chopped roasted
red bell pepper**

**2 tablespoons hummus
(page 142)**

**1 spinach or whole-wheat
flour tortilla, about
8 inches (20 cm) diameter**

Blot the vegetables dry with a paper towel. Spread the hummus evenly over the tortilla, all the way to the edges. Sprinkle the vegetables on top of the hummus, leaving about 1 inch (2.5 cm) uncovered on one side. Starting on the vegetable-covered side, roll up the tortilla into a tight cylinder (the exposed hummus will act as a glue to hold the cylinder together).

Trim the ends, and then slice the cylinder crosswise into pinwheels.

PACK & STORE IT Roll the sliced cylinder in plastic wrap or aluminum foil, folding the ends over to keep it secure. Or, arrange pinwheels, one cut side down, in a parchment paper–lined airtight container. Store in the refrigerator until ready to go, up to 1 day.

almond-banana pinwheels

MAKES ABOUT 8 PINWHEELS

**2 tablespoons
almond butter**

**1 whole-wheat flour
tortilla, about 8 inches
(20 cm) diameter**

½ banana, thinly sliced

Spread the almond butter evenly over the tortilla, all the way to the edges. Arrange the banana slices on top of the almond butter, leaving about 1 inch (2.5 cm) uncovered on one side. Starting on the banana-covered side, roll up the tortilla into a tight cylinder (the exposed almond butter will act as a glue to hold the cylinder together).

Trim the ends, and then slice the cylinder crosswise into pinwheels.

PACK & STORE IT Roll the sliced cylinder in plastic wrap or aluminum foil, folding the ends over to keep it secure. Or, arrange pinwheels, one cut side down, in a parchment paper–lined airtight container. Store in the refrigerator until ready to go, up to 1 day.

turkey & avocado pinwheels

Smoked turkey, creamy avocado, and melted havarti combine to make a protein-packed meal. Avocado adds folate, vitamin E, and plenty of good fat, which is an essential part of every toddler's diet. When the cheese cools, it holds everything together. If smoked turkey prompts a wrinkled nose from your toddler, use milder roasted turkey.

MAKES ABOUT 8 PINWHEELS

1 spinach or whole-wheat flour tortilla, about 8 inches (20 cm) diameter

1 oz (30 g) havarti cheese, thinly sliced or shredded

1½–2 oz (30–45g) smoked or roasted turkey, thinly sliced

¼ avocado, peeled and mashed

Preheat the oven to 350°F (180°C).

Place the tortilla on a baking sheet. Arrange the cheese in an even layer on the tortilla, tearing it into pieces if necessary. Bake until the cheese melts, about 5 minutes.

Arrange the turkey slices over the cheese, leaving about 1 inch (2.5 cm) uncovered on one side. Spread the avocado over the turkey. Starting on the turkey-covered side, roll up the tortilla into a tight cylinder (the exposed melted cheese will act as a glue to hold the cylinder together).

Trim the ends, and then slice the cylinder crosswise into pinwheels.

PACK & STORE IT Roll the sliced cylinder in plastic wrap or aluminum foil, folding the ends over to keep it secure. Or, arrange pinwheels, one cut side down, in a parchment paper–lined airtight container. Store in the refrigerator until ready to go, up to 1 day.

salmon & cucumber pinwheels

There are two great things about pinwheels: they are easy to transport—just roll the cylinder in plastic wrap, place it and a plastic knife into your bag, and slice as needed—and they look really cool. The latter means that it will be hard for any toddler to resist such a colorful swirl of deliciousness. You can use smoked trout fillet in place of the salmon.

MAKES ABOUT 8 PINWHEELS

1 tablespoon shredded English or Persian cucumber

2 tablespoons cream cheese, at room temperature

1 sheet lavash, preferably whole wheat, or whole-wheat flour tortilla, about 8 inches (20 cm) in diameter

1–2 oz (30–60 g) smoked salmon, thinly sliced and then cut into narrow strips

Blot the shredded cucumber dry with a paper towel.

Spread the cream cheese evenly over the lavash, all the way to the edges. Arrange an even layer of salmon on top of the cheese, leaving about 1 inch (2.5 cm) uncovered on one side. Sprinkle the cucumber over the salmon. Starting on the salmon-covered side, roll up the lavash into a tight cylinder (the exposed cream cheese will act as a glue to hold the cylinder together).

Trim the ends, and then slice the cylinder crosswise into pinwheels.

PACK & STORE IT Roll the sliced cylinder in plastic wrap or aluminum foil, folding the ends over to keep it secure. Or, arrange pinwheels, one cut side down, in a parchment paper–lined airtight container. Store in the refrigerator until ready to go, up to 1 day.

fun with pinwheels

Pinwheels and rolls are not only fun for toddlers to eat but are also ideal meals-on-the-go. To make them even more appealing to your toddler, dress them up with these cute packaging ideas.

paper bands

Choose strips of colorful paper to wrap around the pinwheel cylinder to hold it together for transport. Tighten the band, then secure it with a small piece of clear tape.

roll it up

Preslice the cylinder into pinwheels, roll them up in a piece of waxed paper or parchment, and then tie each end with a colorful ribbon.

boxed lunch

Slice the cylinder into pinwheels and stand them on end in your to-go container. Or stack them alongside sliced fruit or other sides for a complete meal.

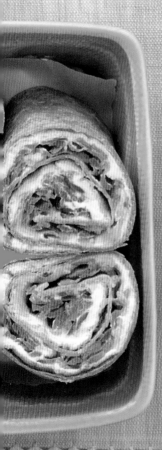

eggplant & ricotta rolls

Not only are these rolls a fun and delicious way to get your toddler to eat more vegetables, but you can also double (or triple) this recipe and serve it to the whole family. Just nestle the eggplant rolls in a baking dish, top with marinara sauce and extra grated Parmesan and bake in a 375°F (190°C) oven until warmed through, about 20 minutes.

MAKES 6 ROLLS

Olive oil cooking spray

1 small Asian eggplant, about 6 oz (175 g)

Kosher salt

⅓ cup (2½ oz/75 g) whole-milk ricotta cheese

¼ cup (1 oz/30 g) finely shredded Parmesan cheese

1 tablespoon finely chopped fresh basil

⅓ cup (3 fl oz/80 ml) purchased marinara sauce

Preheat the oven to 400°F (200°C). Spray a rimmed baking sheet with cooking spray.

Trim the eggplant and cut off a very thin slice lengthwise on each side (to remove excess skin). Slice the eggplant lengthwise into 6 thin slices, each about ¼ inch (6 mm) thick. Lay the slices on the prepared baking sheet, sprinkle with a little salt, and bake, turning once halfway through, until tender and golden, about 12 minutes. Set aside to cool completely.

Meanwhile, in a small bowl, stir together the ricotta, Parmesan, and basil. When the eggplant slices are cool, spread them with the ricotta mixture, dividing it evenly among the slices (about 1 tablespoon per slice). Roll up each eggplant slice into a pinwheel. Serve with the marinara sauce for dipping.

STORE IT Store the rolls in an airtight container in the refrigerator for up to 3 days.

PACK IT Pack 1 or 2 eggplant rolls in an airtight container along with a small container of the marinara sauce.

veggie sushi rolls

Sushi might seem like an ambitious meal to make for your toddler, but once you get the hang of assembling the rolls, it's simple. Plus, these rolls are so delectable that you'll want to double the recipe! Use brown rice to keep things healthy. Try other filling ingredients, too, such as smoked salmon, shredded cooked chicken, or chopped cooked asparagus.

MAKES 8 PIECES

1 cup (5 oz/155 g) cooked brown or white sushi rice

1 teaspoon unseasoned rice vinegar

1 sheet toasted nori seaweed

1 tablespoon toasted sesame seeds

2 tablespoons shredded English cucumber

2 tablespoons shredded carrot

¼ ripe avocado, peeled and thinly sliced

Low-sodium soy sauce and pickled ginger slices for serving (optional)

Place the rice in a microwave-safe bowl, add a few drops of water, and microwave until the rice is warm and softened, about 30 seconds. Set the rice aside to cool slightly.

In a small bowl, combine the vinegar with 2 tablespoons water. Place a bamboo sushi mat on a work surface with the bamboo strips facing you horizontally. Place the nori sheet horizontally, shiny side down, on the mat, aligned with the edge nearest you. Dip your hands into the vinegar-water mixture and spread the cooled rice in an even layer over the nori sheet, leaving the top one-fourth of the nori uncovered. Sprinkle the sesame seeds over the rice, then arrange the cucumber, carrot, and avocado in a horizontal strip across the bottom portion of the rice.

Starting at the edge closest to you, lift the mat, nori, and rice over the filling to seal it inside, then roll up the sushi into a tight cylinder. Use your finger to moisten the far edge of the nori lightly with the vinegar-water mixture to seal the roll. Dipping a sharp knife in water before each cut, cut the roll in half crosswise, and then cut each half crosswise into 4 equal pieces. Accompany the rolls with soy sauce for dipping and pickled ginger, if desired.

PACK & STORE IT Pack the sushi snugly into an airtight container and refrigerate until ready to go, up to 2 days. Include little containers of soy sauce and/or pickled ginger, if your toddler enjoys them.

chicken & veggie rice paper rolls

These fresh spring rolls are a creative way to use up leftover roasted or poached chicken. The wrappers and rice noodles can be found in Southeast Asian groceries and in most well-stocked supermarkets. Look for good-quality prepared peanut sauce that doesn't contain a lot of sugar or salt, or, better yet, make your own favorite recipe.

MAKES 4 ROLLS

1 oz (30 g) rice stick noodles

3 tablespoons shredded cucumber

3 tablespoons shredded carrot

½ cup (3 oz/90 g) shredded cooked chicken

1 tablespoon finely chopped fresh cilantro, basil, or mint

2 teaspoons seasoned rice vinegar

1 teaspoon fresh lime juice

Kosher salt

4 rice paper wrappers, about 8½ inches (21.5 cm) in diameter

Purchased peanut sauce for serving

Place the noodles in a bowl, pour very hot water over them to cover, and let stand until soft, about 10 minutes. Drain. Blot the shredded vegetables dry with paper towels.

In a bowl, toss together the chicken, cucumber, carrot, cilantro, rice vinegar, lime juice, and a pinch of salt.

Fill a 9-inch (23-cm) round cake pan with warm water. One at a time, place a rice paper round into the water, turning it gently with your fingertips until softened. Carefully remove the sheet from the water, and lay it flat on a plate.

Arrange one-fourth each of the noodles and the chicken mixture in a horizontal line on the wrapper, positioning them about 1 inch (2.5 cm) or so from the edge nearest you and about ½ inch (12 mm) from each side. Lift the edge nearest you and place it over the filling, then roll once to form a tight cylinder. Fold in the sides of the rice paper and continue to roll the rice paper and filling to form a cylinder. Repeat with the remaining rice paper and filling.

STORE IT Wrap each rice paper roll in plastic wrap and refrigerate for up to 2 days.

PACK IT Cut 1 roll into pieces and wrap in plastic wrap. Include a small covered container of peanut sauce for dipping, if your toddler enjoys it.

fun with sammies

Sandwiches appeal to even the pickiest of eaters and you can put just about anything inside of them. To keep things fun and interesting, vary the types of bread, the shapes of the sandwiches, and the packaging.

creative packing ideas

Choose different types and shapes of bread.

Cut sammies into creative shapes.

Line to-go containers with boldly patterned paper.

Wrap sammies in colorful paper and tie with a ribbon or twine.

Seal sandwiches in patterned paper bags.

creamy cucumber sammies

MAKES 1 SANDWICH

1 whole-wheat mini bagel

1 tablespoon cream cheese, at room temperature

About 6 thin slices cucumber

Split the bagel and lightly toast the halves. Spread the cut sides of the bagel with the cream cheese, dividing it evenly. Top half of the bagel with a layer of the cucumber slices, then cover with the other bagel half, cheese side down, and press gently.

PACK IT Wrap in plastic wrap, aluminum foil, or parchment paper, or place in a small airtight container.

pepper & goat cheese sammies

MAKES 1 SANDWICH

3-inch (7.5-cm) square focaccia

2 tablespoons fresh goat cheese, at room temperature

¼ cup (1½ oz/45 g) chopped roasted red pepper

Split the focaccia in half crosswise. Spread the cut sides with the goat cheese, dividing it evenly. Top half of the focaccia with a layer of the roasted red pepper, then cover with the other focaccia half, cheese side down, and press gently.

PACK IT Wrap in plastic wrap, aluminum foil, or parchment paper, or place in a small airtight container.

cashew butter & jam sammies

MAKES 1 SANDWICH

1 English muffin

1 tablespoon cashew butter

1 tablespoon favorite jam

Split the muffin. Spread the cut side of half of the muffin with the cashew butter and the cut side of the other half with the jam. Put the cut sides together, pressing gently.

NOTE Instead of cashew butter, try almond butter or sunflower-seed butter. Or, swap out the muffin for a homemade biscuit.

PACK IT Wrap in plastic wrap, aluminum foil, or parchment paper, or place in a small airtight container.

peanut-apple-cheddar sammies

MAKES 1 SANDWICH

2 thin slices whole-wheat bread

1–2 tablespoons peanut butter

About 3 thin slices Cheddar cheese

About 6 thin slices apple

Spread one side of both bread slices with the peanut butter, dividing it evenly. Top 1 peanut butter–covered bread slice with an even layer of the cheese slices, and then the apple slices. Cover with the other bread slice, peanut butter side down, and press gently. Using a sandwich cutter or a cookie cutter, press down firmly on the sandwich to cut it into shapes. Discard (or snack on) the scraps.

NOTE Cutting sandwiches into fun shapes makes them even more appealing to toddlers. Try triangles or "sticks," or use a star-shaped or heart-shaped cookie cutter.

PACK IT Wrap in plastic wrap, aluminum foil, or parchment paper, or place in a small airtight container.

fish sammies

This sandwich takes tuna salad to new flavor heights, with crunchy celery and tart green apple, and a sprinkle of parsley and lemon juice. Tuna is an excellent source of lean protein, omega-3 fatty acids, and selenium. Leftover cooked salmon or canned salmon makes a delicious substitute for the tuna.

MAKES 1 SANDWICH

1 whole-wheat mini bagel

1 can (5 oz/155 g) water-packed white albacore tuna or salmon, drained

2 teaspoons finely chopped celery

2 tablespoons shredded green apple

1 tablespoon finely chopped fresh flat-leaf parsley

1 teaspoon fresh lemon juice

About 2 tablespoons mayonnaise

Split the bagel and lightly toast the halves.

In a bowl, combine the tuna, celery, apple, parsley, lemon juice, and just enough mayonnaise to bind together all of the ingredients. Stir until well mixed. Pile some of the tuna mixture onto the bagel bottom. Cover with the bagel top and press gently.

NOTE You will have more tuna salad than you need. Refrigerate the remainder in an airtight container for up to 2 days. Use for additional sandwiches or as a snack with whole-grain crackers later in the week.

PACK IT Wrap in plastic wrap, aluminum foil, or parchment paper, or place in a small airtight container.

artichoke dip sammies

Here is a sandwich with plenty of nutritional pluses: the tangy artichoke hearts are high in antioxidants, the spinach is packed with vitamins and minerals, and the whole-wheat roll is rich in fiber, vitamin E, folate, and manganese. The creamy filling acts as a glue to hold the sandwich together, making it perfect for on-the-go meals.

MAKES 1 SANDWICH

¼ cup (2 oz/60 g) finely chopped marinated artichoke hearts

1 tablespoon cream cheese, at room temperature

1 tablespoon finely grated Parmesan cheese

2 teaspoons mayonnaise

2 tablespoons very finely chopped baby spinach leaves

1 whole-wheat dinner roll, split

In a bowl, combine the artichoke hearts, cream cheese, Parmesan cheese, mayonnaise, and spinach. Stir until well mixed.

Pile some of the artichoke mixture onto the bottom half of the roll. Cover with the roll top and press gently.

NOTE You will have more artichoke dip than you need. Refrigerate the remainder in an airtight container for up to 3 days. Use for additional sandwiches or as a snack with whole-grain crackers later in the week.

PACK IT Wrap in plastic wrap, aluminum foil, or parchment paper, or place in a small airtight container.

turkey, brie & jam sammies

MAKES 1 SANDWICH

1 whole-wheat English muffin

2 tablespoons Brie cheese, at room temperature

1 slice roasted turkey breast

2 teaspoons favorite jam

Split the muffin and lightly toast the halves.

Spread the cut sides of the muffin with the Brie, dividing it evenly. Top half of the muffin with the turkey slice, then spread the other half with a thin layer of jam. Put the halves together and press gently.

PACK IT Wrap in plastic wrap, aluminum foil, or parchment paper, or place in a small airtight container.

pesto & mozzarella sammies

MAKES 1 SANDWICH

2 thin slices sourdough bread

1–2 tablespoons purchased fresh basil pesto

4 thin slices fresh mozzarella cheese

Spread one side of both bread slices with the pesto, dividing it evenly. Top 1 pesto-covered bread slice with the mozzarella. Cover with the other pesto-covered slice, pesto side down, and press gently. Cut into squares or triangles.

NOTE Pesto often contains nuts such as pine nuts or walnuts. Be certain that your toddler does not have a nut allergy before adding pesto to a meal.

PACK IT Wrap in plastic wrap, aluminum foil, or parchment paper, or place in a small airtight container.

mini pita pockets

Choose mini pita breads, about 3 inches (7.5 cm) in diameter
and preferably whole wheat, for each of these fun sandwiches.
Split the pita, leaving about half intact so it will hold together
during transport. You can also use these same sandwich fillings
with any sliced multigrain bread or whole-wheat rolls.

baby bahn mi

In a bowl, stir together ¼ cup (1½ oz/45 g)
shredded braised pork (page 41),
1 tablespoon each shredded cucumber
and carrot, 1 teaspoon chopped fresh cilantro,
1 tablespoon finely diced mango, and
2 teaspoons mayonnaise. Stuff into
the pita and close tightly.

chicken salad

In a bowl, stir together ¼ cup
(1½ oz/45 g) shredded cooked chicken
(page 41), 2 tablespoons chopped grapes,
1 tablespoon chopped roasted red pepper,
1 teaspoon finely chopped fresh mint,
and 2 teaspoons mayonnaise.
Stuff into the pita and close tightly.

caprese

Layer the following ingredients inside the pita: 2 thin slices fresh mozzarella; ½ teaspoon finely chopped fresh basil; 2 tablespoons shredded cucumber, blotted dry with a paper towel; ¼ avocado, sliced; and 2 tablespoons chopped cherry tomatoes.

meatball

Slice 1 meatball (page 82) and layer it inside the pita. Stir together 1 tablespoon finely diced tomatoes, 1 tablespoon chopped cooked spinach, and 1 tablespoon plain whole-milk Greek yogurt; dollop into the pita and close tightly.

avocado toasties

MAKES 1 SANDWICH

2 thin slices multigrain bread

½ ripe avocado, peeled

Fresh lemon juice

Kosher salt

Lightly toast the bread. In a bowl, mash together the avocado, a squeeze of lemon juice, and a small pinch of salt. Spread one side of both bread slices with the mashed avocado, dividing it evenly. Put the bread slices together and press gently. Cut into squares or triangles.

NOTE When you are on the go, it's best (and less messy) if you serve these as a closed sandwich. But when you are home, you can serve them to your little one as open-faced toasts.

PACK IT Wrap in plastic wrap, aluminum foil, or parchment paper, or place in a small airtight container.

mini grilled cheddar & veggies

MAKES 3 MINI SANDWICHES

3 tablespoons finely shredded Cheddar cheese

1 tablespoon shredded carrot

1 tablespoon shredded zucchini

1 tablespoon finely chopped baby spinach

6 thin slices baguette

1 teaspoon unsalted butter, at room temperature

In a bowl, toss together the cheese, carrot, zucchini, and spinach.

Spread one side of each baguette slice with a little butter. On three of the unbuttered sides, mound the cheese mixture. Top with the remaining baguette slices, unbuttered side down, and press gently.

Warm a small, nonstick frying pan over medium heat. Add the assembled sandwiches and toast, turning and pressing on the sandwiches with the back of a spatula, until crisp and golden brown, the cheese is melted, and the vegetables are tender, about 5 minutes. Let cool completely.

PACK IT Wrap in plastic wrap, aluminum foil, or parchment paper, or place in a small airtight container.

DIPS & DIPPERS

a wholesome meal

Plunging food into a delicious dip is an endless source of fun for little ones and is one of the few times you might let your child play with his food! And while some toddlers might shy away from sauces on their food, dipping vegetable chunks, sliced fruits, or whole-grain breads into tasty purees and wholesome dips is a great way to keep their interest when they are eating, especially if you offer them a variety of easy-to-grasp dippers.

Although dips and dippers make a great snack any time of day, they can also easily be made into a well-balanced meal. For example, bean dips offer protein and fiber, and yogurt and cheese dips deliver calcium. When you pair such dips with fresh vegetable, fruit, or whole-grain dippers, you can be sure that your child is getting essential vitamins and minerals.

A dips & dippers toolkit

Dips and dippers are easy to make and require just a few everyday kitchen tools.

Blender or food processor for pureeing

Rubber spatula for scraping

Fork for mashing; spoon for mixing

Large knife for slicing and chopping

Large saucepan for cooking vegetables

Colander for draining and cooling cooked vegetables

Frying pan for sautéing

Easy peasy

The dips in this chapter are incredibly quick and easy to prepare. Most of them call for simply tossing a few ingredients into a blender or food processor and whizzing them to a smooth consistency. That's it! Many dippers can be prepped in advance and stored in an airtight container in the refrigerator, so that all you have to do is pop a few into a container, grab a dip, and away you go. Many of these dips (without the dippers) can also be fed to babies and added to your repertoire of purees when they are 6 to 12 months old. However, take care to first check the ingredient list and the information on page 18 to be sure they won't cause an allergic reaction in your tot.

Storing Dips

Most of the dip recipes in this chapter make enough for two to four servings and will keep in the refrigerator for 3 days or 1 week. The exceptions are the Guacamole (page 145), Cucumber-Yogurt Dip (page 146), and Fruit & Vanilla Yogurt Dip (page 151), all of which should be made and used within 1 day.

The following dips from this book can be frozen for up to 3 months: Black Bean Dip (page 141);

White Bean Dip (page 141); Hummus (page 142); Roasted Pepper & Goat Cheese Dip (page 146); Ranch-Style Dip (page 148); Creamy Onion Dip (page 149); and Spiced Nut Butter Dip (page 151).

If you prepare a dip that can be frozen, refrigerate enough for one or two meals in the coming days, then freeze the rest:

- Divide the remaining dip into individual portions. I like to use reusable small plastic containers with airtight lids. You can also use small baby-food freezer containers, but don't use glass, as it can crack.

- Freeze until firm, at least 2 hours.

- To thaw a dip, place it in the refrigerator for at least 24 hours before you want to serve it. Never thaw food at room temperature.

- Once you have thawed a frozen dip, do not refreeze it. Refrigerate it and use within 2 days.

Tips for dips

In addition to the dip recipes in this chapter, there are lots of premade dipping options at the supermarket that you can purchase in a pinch. Try to choose dips or sauces that are made without sugar, preservatives, or additives. My daughter's favorites include Asian-style peanut sauce, basil pesto, marinara sauce, mild tomato salsa, mild tomatillo salsa, peanut butter and other nut butters, and plain, whole-milk yogurt. Paired with fresh vegetables (see page 138 for ideas), these purchased dips make wholesome snacks or they can be combined with other foods to make a nourishing meal.

Choose dippers wisely

If your toddler enjoys vegetables as dippers, take care when serving firm ones, which can be difficult for little teeth to chew and can be a choking hazard. If serving broccoli, cauliflower, carrots, or asparagus, be sure to cook them first (below) to make sure they are soft enough for your toddler. Other vegetables, such as sugar snap peas, or green beans, can also be partially or completely cooked to make them more toothsome for your toddler.

Preparing Vegetables

Vegetable dippers often need to be cooked to soften their texture. Vegetables can be cooked up to 3 days in advance and stored in the refrigerator (for a list of dippers, see page 138).

To cook vegetables Bring a saucepan of lightly salted water to a boil. Add the vegetables and simmer until just tender. This can take as little as 2 or 3 minutes or up to about 8 minutes, depending on the vegetable. Drain in a colander and rinse under cold running water.

To store vegetables Once the vegetables have cooled to room temperature, store them in an airtight container in the refrigerator for up to 3 days. To use, simply pull out whatever you need for a meal and place in an individual container for easy transport.

all about dippers

Healthful dips and dippers are a great way to turn a popular snack into a wholesome mini meal. Offer any of the following dippers—depending on what your toddler likes and can handle—along with the dips found in this chapter, or with plain whole-milk yogurt or purchased hummus.

grain dippers

toasted whole-wheat
mini pitas, quartered

whole-wheat bread or toast,
cut into "sticks"

whole-wheat tortillas,
cut into bite-sized pieces

cooked polenta, spread in a dish,
cooled, and cut into bite-sized pieces

multigrain crackers

fruit dippers

dried apricots or mangoes,
cut into bite-sized pieces

grapes, halved

peaches or nectarines, sliced

strawberries, quartered

vegetable dippers

roasted red bell pepper strips

broccoli florets, cooked

cauliflower florets, cooked

baby carrot sticks,
cooked and quartered

cherry tomatoes, quartered

sugar snap peas, cooked,
and halved

zucchini sticks, cooked

green beans, cooked, and halved

asparagus spears,
cooked and chopped

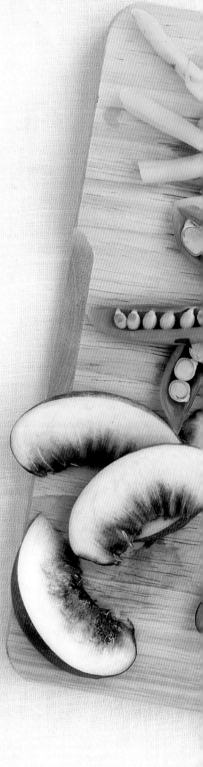

black bean dip

MAKES ABOUT 2 CUPS (1 LB/500 G)

1 can (15 oz/470 g) black beans, rinsed and drained

1 small tomato, chopped

2 teaspoons fresh cilantro leaves

½ teaspoon ground cumin

2 teaspoons fresh lime juice

Kosher salt and freshly ground pepper

1 tablespoon olive oil

In a blender or food processor, combine the beans, tomato, cilantro, cumin, lime juice, and a pinch each of salt and pepper. Process until smooth, occasionally scraping down the sides. With the machine running, slowly pour in the oil. Blend until the mixture is very smooth. Add a little water if necessary to thin the mixture slightly.

DIP IT Try multigrain toast, whole-wheat or corn tortillas, roasted red bell peppers, halved cherry tomatoes, or cooked zucchini sticks.

STORE IT Refrigerate in an airtight container for up to 1 week.

PACK IT Pack the dip and dippers in separate covered containers.

white bean dip

MAKES ABOUT 2 CUPS (1 LB/500 G)

1 can (15 oz/470 g) cannellini beans, rinsed and drained

½ small shallot, chopped

¼ teaspoon fresh thyme leaves

2 teaspoons fresh lemon juice

Kosher salt and freshly ground pepper

2 tablespoons olive oil

In a blender or food processor, combine the beans, shallot, thyme, lemon juice, and a pinch each of salt and pepper. Blend until smooth, occasionally scraping down the sides. With the machine running, slowly pour in the oil. Blend until the mixture is very smooth. Add a little water if necessary to thin the mixture slightly.

DIP IT Try cooked asparagus spears, baby carrot sticks, or sugar snap peas; cooked polenta bites; or multigrain crackers.

STORE IT Refrigerate in an airtight container for up to 1 week.

PACK IT Pack the dip and dippers in separate covered containers.

hummus

Lemony hummus is a protein-rich dip or spread that is as delicious as it is good for baby. Easy to make—just whirl all of the ingredients in a blender—and versatile, it can be served with whole-wheat pita, wholegrain crackers, cooked vegetable sticks, or mini bagels. Experiment with the flavor by adding roasted red bell peppers or avocado to the blender.

MAKES ABOUT 2 CUPS (1 LB/500 G)

1 can (15 oz/470 g) chickpeas, rinsed and drained

⅓ cup (3½ oz/105 g) tahini (sesame paste)

¼ teaspoon minced garlic (optional)

Juice of 1 large lemon

½ teaspoon ground cumin

2 tablespoons olive oil

¼ teaspoon sweet paprika, plus more for garnish (optional)

In a blender or food processor, combine the chickpeas, tahini, garlic (if using), lemon juice, and cumin and process until smooth, occasionally scraping down the sides. With the machine running, slowly pour in the oil. Blend until the mixture is very smooth. Add a little water if necessary to thin the mixture to a dippable consistency. When you serve it, dust the top with a tiny pinch of paprika, if desired.

DIP IT Try cooked carrot sticks; red bell pepper strips; halved cherry or pear tomatoes; whole-wheat mini pita; or toast.

STORE IT Refrigerate in an airtight container for up to 1 week.

PACK IT Pack the dip and dippers in separate covered containers.

guacamole

Avocados are a great on-the-go food for babies and toddlers; just toss one into your bag and mash it to the perfect consistency wherever you are. But turning it into guacamole makes it even more delicious. Try adding a little pinch of cayenne or minced jalapeño. I was surprised when my daughter ate a huge helping of spicy guacamole at only 10 months.

MAKES ABOUT ¾ CUP (6 OZ/185 G)

1 avocado

1 tablespoon fresh cilantro leaves, finely chopped

2 teaspoons fresh lime juice

1 tablespoon plain whole-milk yogurt

Kosher salt

Cut the avocado in half lengthwise and remove the pit. Use a spoon to scoop out the flesh into a bowl, discarding the skin. Using a fork, mash the avocado until smooth. Add the cilantro, lime juice, and yogurt and beat with the fork until smooth and creamy. Season to taste with salt.

DIP IT Try corn or whole-wheat tortilla strips; halved cherry tomatoes; or cooked baby carrot or zucchini sticks.

STORE IT Refrigerate in an airtight container for up to 1 day.

PACK IT Pack the dip and dippers in separate covered containers.

cucumber-yogurt dip

MAKES ABOUT ¾ CUP (6 OZ/185 G)

½ cup (4 oz/125 g)
plain whole-milk yogurt

2 tablespoons finely
shredded English
cucumber

½ teaspoon finely
chopped fresh mint

1 teaspoon fresh
lemon juice

Kosher salt

In a bowl, stir together the yogurt, cucumber, mint, and lemon juice. Season to taste with salt.

DIP IT Try cooked broccoli florets or asparagus spears; halved cherry tomatoes; or whole-grain toast strips.

STORE IT Refrigerate in an airtight container for up to 3 days.

PACK IT Pack the dip and dippers in separate covered containers.

red pepper & goat cheese dip

MAKES ABOUT ¾ CUP (6 OZ/185 G)

⅓ cup (2 oz/60 g) roasted
red bell peppers, chopped

¼ cup (1½ oz/45 g) fresh
goat cheese

3 tablespoons silken tofu

1–2 teaspoons fresh
lemon juice

Kosher salt

In a food processor or blender, process the roasted peppers until smooth. Add the goat cheese, tofu, and lemon juice and process until the mixture is well blended. Refrigerate for about 1 hour to thicken.

DIP IT Try cooked cauliflower florets, green beans, or sugar snap peas; or multigrain crackers.

STORE IT Refrigerate in an airtight container for up to 1 week.

PACK IT Pack the dip and dippers in separate covered containers.

ranch-style dip

When I was a kid, I loved eating green salads with ranch dressing, and I wanted to find a way to turn the flavors of that creamy classic into a healthy dip for toddlers. In place of the buttermilk, sour cream, and mayonnaise, I use whole-milk yogurt and cottage cheese. The result is just as delicious as the original and carries plenty of calcium and protein.

MAKES ABOUT ¾ CUP (6 OZ/185 G)

½ cup (4 oz/125 g) plain whole-milk yogurt

¼ cup (2 oz/60 g) cottage cheese

½ teaspoon rice vinegar

¼ teaspoon chopped fresh dill

1 teaspoon chopped fresh flat-leaf parsley leaves

1 teaspoon chopped fresh chives

⅛ teaspoon minced garlic (optional)

Sugar

Kosher salt and freshly ground pepper

In a blender or food processor, combine the yogurt, cottage cheese, vinegar, dill, parsley, chives, garlic (if using), and a small pinch each of sugar, salt, and pepper. Process until smooth and creamy, occasionally scraping down the sides.

DIP IT Try cooked broccoli or cauliflower florets, green beans, or zucchini sticks; or whole-wheat mini pitas.

STORE IT Refrigerate in an airtight container for up to 3 days.

PACK IT Pack the dip and dippers in separate covered containers.

creamy onion dip

This dip is so good that you'll want to make an extra batch to serve at your next adult get-together. Sweet caramelized onion appeals to just about every eater, finicky or not. When you stir it into a creamy mixture of yogurt and mayonnaise, you end up with a dip that your toddler will happily scoop up with healthful vegetable sticks or crackers.

MAKES ABOUT ¾ CUP (6 OZ/185 G)

1 teaspoon olive oil

½ cup (2½ oz/75 g) yellow onion, finely chopped

Kosher salt and freshly ground pepper

¼ cup (2 oz/60 g) plain whole-milk yogurt

1 tablespoon mayonnaise

1 teaspoon finely chopped fresh flat-leaf parsley

Garlic powder

In a frying pan over medium heat, warm the oil. Add the onion and a small pinch of salt and sauté, stirring occasionally, until caramelized, about 20 minutes. Set aside to cool.

In a bowl, stir together the yogurt, mayonnaise, parsley, and a pinch each of garlic powder, salt, and pepper. Stir in the reserved onion.

DIP IT Try cooked broccoli florets, asparagus spears, or baby carrot sticks; whole-wheat bread; or multigrain crackers.

STORE IT Refrigerate in an airtight container for up to 3 days.

PACK IT Pack the dip and dippers in separate covered containers.

fruit & vanilla yogurt dip

MAKES ABOUT ½ CUP (4 OZ/125 G)

⅓ cup (2½ oz/75 g) plain whole-milk yogurt

¼ teaspoon pure vanilla extract

2 tablespoons jam or preserves, such as fig, apricot, or sour cherry, or your toddler's favorite

In a bowl, combine the yogurt, vanilla, and jam and stir until well mixed.

DIP IT Try sliced peaches or nectarines, quartered strawberries, or halved grapes.

STORE IT Refrigerate in an airtight container for up to 1 day.

PACK IT Pack the dip and dippers in separate covered containers.

spiced nut butter dip

MAKES ABOUT ½ CUP (4 OZ/125 G)

¼ cup (2½ oz/75 g) almond or cashew butter with no added sugar

2 teaspoons honey

¼ cup (2 oz/60 g) plain whole-milk yogurt

Pinch of ground cinnamon

Pinch of ground allspice

In a bowl, combine the nut butter and honey and stir until smooth. Add the yogurt, cinnamon, and allspice and stir until well mixed.

NOTE Honey is not recommended for babies under 1 year of age.

DIP IT Try cooked baby carrot sticks, ripe pear slices, multigrain toast, or whole-wheat mini pita.

STORE IT Refrigerate in an airtight container for up to 1 week.

PACK IT Pack the dip and dippers in separate covered containers.

cottage cheese mix-ins

Cottage cheese is a great way to give your toddler both protein and calcium, but it can be boring on its own. Gussy it up by stirring 1–3 tablespoons of any of these mix-ins into ⅓ cup (3 oz/90 g) whole-milk cottage cheese.

unsweetened applesauce

diced or mashed ripe nectarine or banana

finely chopped pineapple, mango, or cantaloupe

pumpkin puree with a pinch of cinnamon

finely chopped dried fruit
such as raisins, dates, or apricots

finely chopped ham

shredded cucumber

chopped roasted red bell pepper

chopped cooked spinach

Index

weldonowen

415 Jackson Street, Suite 200, San Francisco, CA 94111
www.weldonowen.com

Weldon Owen is a division of
BONNIER

WELDON OWEN, INC.

CEO and President Terry Newell
VP, Sales and Marketing Amy Kaneko
Director of Finance Mark Perrigo

VP and Publisher Hannah Rahill
Executive Editor Jennifer Newens

Creative Director Emma Boys
Senior Art Director Kara Church
Designer Rachel Lopez Metzger

Production Director Chris Hemesath
Production Manager Michelle Duggan

Photographer Thayer Allyson Gowdy
Food Stylist Erin Quan
Prop Stylist Esther Feinman
Illustrator Lorena Siminovich

BABY & TODDLER ON THE GO

Conceived and produced by Weldon Owen, Inc.
Copyright © 2013 Weldon Owen, Inc.

All rights reserved, including the right of reproduction in whole or in part in any form.

Printed and bound by 1010 Printing in China

First printed in 2013
10 9 8 7 6 5 4 3 2 1

Library of Congress Control Number: 2012956029

ISBN13: 978-1-61628-499-2
ISBN 10: 1-61628-499-4

ACKNOWLEDGMENTS

From Kim Laidlaw: I owe so much gratitude to both my husband and our daughter Poppy, without whom I couldn't have written this book. My husband's patience and support kept me going, and my toddler-with-a-big-appetite tried every single recipe in this book (my husband tried many of them as well!). An extra big thank you to all my baby and toddler taste testers—Sophie, Beatrix, Mila, and Alice—who offered their honest feedback by either gobbling up the food or spitting it out, and their awesome moms who tested recipes and gave me invaluable feedback along the way.

Weldon Owen wishes to thank the following people for their generous support in producing this book:
Jaime Beechum, Eve Lynch, Lori Nunokawa, and Sharon Silva.

PHOTO CREDITS
All photos by Thayer Allyson Gowdy except: page 12 and 52 by Ericka McConnell